Russian Orthodox Liturgical Performance Practice

Father Andrei Papkov

**Aleksandr Andreev,
Translator**

Russian Orthodox Liturgical Performance Practice

Father Andrei Papkov

Aleksandr Andreev,
Translator

Academica Press
Washington~London

Library of Congress Cataloging-in-Publication Data

Names: Papkov, Andrei. (author)
Title: Russian orthodox liturgical performance practice | Papkov, Andrei
Description: Washington : Academica Press, 2023. | Includes references.
Identifiers: LCCN 2023941381 | ISBN 9781680536393 (hardcover) | 9781680536416 (e-book) | 9781680536409 (paperback)

Copyright 2023 Andrei Papkov

Holy Dormition Convent (Novo-Diveyevo)

2023 edition

By Archpriest Andrei Papkov

Translated by A. A. Andreev

Editors: A. V. Shipovalnikov,
P. A. Fekula, V. V. Krasovsky, and I. A. du Quenoy

Contents

Preface xi

Part I: Theory 1

§ 1 About the Cliros Library – Liturgical Books 1

§ 2 The Cliros Library – Anthologies of Sheet Music 6

§ 3 Reading on the Cliros 11

§ 4 Kievan Square Notation 14

§ 5 Singing to the Tonal Melodies 19

§ 6 "Clerical Harmonization" 26

§ 7 About Singing Recitative 30

§ 8 The Choice of Liturgical Repertoire 32

§ 9 The Choice of Repertoire: The Influence of Music on a Person 39

§ 10 On Diversity in the Services 41

§ 11 Concerning Abbreviations in Liturgical Practice 45

§ 12 The Element of Time in the Services 52

§ 13 The Relationship between the Choir Director and the Rector 55

Part II: Practical Considerations 59

§ 14 Some Information about the Vocal Apparatus 59

§ 15 On the Speaking and Singing Positions of the Vocal Apparatus .. 61

§ 16 Timbre 61

§ 17 Some Tips for Rehearsing the Choir 62

§ 18 Notes of an Experienced Choir Director 66

§ 19 Difficulties with an Amateur Choir 68

§ 20 About "Tone-Deaf" Clergy 70

§ 21 About Bell Ringing 71
§ 22 Conclusion 72

Appendix 1:
The Bakhmetev Obikhod Title Page 73

Appendix 2:
Bakhmetev Obikhod sample page 75

Appendix 3:
Dogmatic Theotokia in the eight tones,
Znamenny chant (square notation) 77

Appendix 4:
Cheat Sheet 85

Appendix 5:
Podobny/Automela 87

Appendix 6:
The Eight Tones – Monophonic Obikhod 111

Appendix 7:
Melodies for "It is truly meet" 164

Appendix 8:
The Typicon on "Disorderly Shrieks" and other commentary ... 169

Appendix 9:
Vowel formation chart 173

Appendix 10:
On breath control 175

Appendix 11:
Some websites with liturgical music 177

Appendix 12:
On bell ringing: Fr. Seraphim Slobodskoy and N. V. Matveev ... 179

Preface

This set of lecture notes has been compiled with the aim of helping people who have come to the church choir (*cliros*), often an unfamiliar environment, and asked to carry out a quite unfamiliar task. These individuals, in most cases volunteers, usually come to church from a variety of vocations and professions, and the degree of their preparation and suitability for singing and reading at church services is quite varied. They are united by one set of circumstances: they all need help in a particular area of work in the field of liturgical performance practice. In offering the material compiled here, we sought to touch upon those facets of church music that they will inevitably encounter in their service, and in which they cannot orient themselves without outside help because often they do not even suspect the existence of many such facets of liturgical performance practice. In writing out these lecture notes, we touched upon those aspects of cliros service that we believe are particularly worthy of attention. This belief is based on our observations over half a century of experience on the cliros. These lecture notes do not claim to be comprehensive, since church singing is a lively, dynamic activity, one that does not stand still. At any time, unexpected situations may arise that are not provided for here and that require a solution at the local level.

The textbook has been compiled on the basis of questions asked by students of the Liturgical Performance Practice class at the Synodal School of Liturgical Music over a period of thirty years. Often, the same questions would arise, and so we may reasonably expect that they will arise in the future. Still, it is not possible for us to predict all new questions that may arise over time. Therefore, we ask the kind reader to help us and point out things that we may have missed, should they find them. We anticipate expanding and editing this textbook in the future and would be grateful for any constructive feedback.

Archpriest Andrei Papkov

Part I:

Theory

§ 1
About the Cliros Library – Liturgical Books

To successfully conduct services, the Choir Director / Precentor must have on hand all the necessary liturgical books, which include:

1. **The Horologion**: Contains all the unchanging prayers of the daily cycle of divine services and, according to the ever-memorable Archimandrite Sergius (Romberg), is the canvas on which the beautiful embroidery of other (variable) liturgical texts is laid out. There are several editions of the Horologion, both domestic and foreign, both pre-revolutionary and newer, more or less successfully compiled.

The most convenient to use and therefore, recommended by us, is the *YMCA Prayer Book*, published by this organization in Paris after World War II.

This edition is in wide use, given the its convenient nature. It appears (based on the differences in book binding and the quality of the paper) that the Parisian publishers reprinted it several times. It was also reprinted by the Convent of Our Lady of Vladimir (ROCOR) prior to their departure into schism.

This version of the Horologion contains the order of the Divine Liturgy, which is rare for other publications of this type, even the prerevolutionary Russian ones. It includes the weekly antiphons ("It is good to give praise unto the Lord, etc."), which makes it possible to serve the Liturgy on weekdays according to the Typicon. Psalm 33 is also placed in its proper location. In addition, the selection of Troparia and Kontakia collected at the end of the book is compiled in such a way that it minimizes the need to use other books – Menaia, Triodia, and the Octoechos.

2. **The Octoechos** – a two-volume collection, containing the cycle of weekday services in the eight tones. The first part contains Tones 1 through 4 and the second part Tones 5 through 8.

During the liturgical year the texts of the Octoechos are usually combined in the prescribed manner with a succession of daily texts contained in the Menaion.

3. **The Menaion** – a twelve-volume collection corresponding to the twelve months of the year, which provides services for every day of the year in honor of the saints or other sacred events (the annual fixed circle of worship).

4. **Lenten Triodion** – Contains liturgical services for Lent and the preparatory weeks. The first service of the Lenten Triodion is Vespers on the eve of the Sunday of the Publican and the Pharisee, the last service—Vespers on the evening of Holy Saturday. The end of the book contains a succession of liturgical material as an appendix:

a) Triadica in the eight tones,
b) Sessional Hymns from the Ochtoechos
c) The "History of the Acathist"
d) Mark's Chapters (liturgical instructions)

5. **The Flowery Triodion (Pentecostarion)** – Contains liturgical texts for the Pentecostarion period, starting from the Paschal Matins (before the procession) with the singing of "Thy Resurrection, O Christ our Savior," and concluding with the end of the Matins for the Sunday of All Saints. At the end as an appendix we find:

a) The Three-Ode Canons for the Pentecostarion Period
b) The Mark's Chapters

Both the Lenten and Flowery Triodia contain the texts for the movable worship cycle, which depends on the date of Easter (Pascha); the Triodia are used in services consecutively (Lenten, then Flowery) over the course of four months.

6. **The Psalter** – The collection of Psalms of the Prophet and King David, which largely formed the basis of our Orthodox hymnography. The 150 Psalms placed in the Psalter are divided into 20 cathismata for more convenient liturgical use.

The number of psalms in each cathisma is not equal. For example, Cathisma 17 contains only one psalm, Psalm 118, whereas Cathisma 18 contains fifteen psalms. The average number is around 8 to 9 psalms per cathisma. The length of the psalms is also uneven (e.g., Psalm 118 has 176 verses, whereas Psalm 116 has 2 verses). Besides the psalms, the Psalter also contains the redaction of the Biblical Odes that is sung at the weekday services of Great Lent.

7. **Liturgical Epistle Book** – Contains the epistle lessons read at the Liturgy. When serving the Liturgy with two or more deacons, the senior deacon reads the Holy Gospel and the junior deacon reads the Epistle. Since this situation is relatively rare, especially in during the weekday services, most often the epistle lesson is read by the Reader / Precentor, and so the book should be kept in the choir. In the altar, another liturgical Epistle book is stored for the use of the deacon.

The book contains the Acts of the Apostles and all of their epistles for liturgical reading. Besides the fact that each epistle is divided into chapters according to the division of the Bible, in the liturgical book the epistles are divided into specific fragments called "pericopes" for more convenient liturgical use. A total of 335 liturgical pericopes exist in the Epistle Book, which are numbered consecutively throughout the entire book (unlike the pericopes of the Gospel). In addition, the end of the book contains:

a) The summary of Antiphons and Prokeimena—instruction on what p prokimena and which readings are used throughout the liturgical year, from Pascha until Holy Saturday. This section of the book also provides a number of important liturgical directives for the daily Epistle readings throughout the year.

b) A Menologion for 12 months, with instructions on Epistle lessons and their prokimena and Alleluias for the annual festive circle.

c) Prokimena and Alleluia for:

1. Sunday

2. Weekdays

3. General categories of saints

4. For different needs.

8. **Great Compendium** — (applicable only for use in Church Slavonic services, as it is does not exist in English). This is a unique edition that deserves special mention. Because of the military and political upheavals of the twentieth century, the parishes of the Russian Orthodox Church Outside of Russia suffered from a lack of liturgical books. Until the middle of the century, it was still possible to procure such books from Russian monasteries on the Holy Mountain, but over time this source (never abundant) dried up for various reasons. The acute need for liturgical books was felt even in the years before World War II.

The Printing Brotherhood of St. Job of Pochaev in Ladomirovo in the Carpathian Mountains, with the blessing of Archbishop Vitaly (Maksimenko), started to publish the *Great Compendium*, a liturgical anthology, to fill this gap. The first edition of this book was printed a few years before the war. Since the books did not have time to spread to parishes across various countries of the diaspora due to the hostilities in Europe, the brotherhood launched the second edition after their move to the Holy Trinity Monastery in Jordanville, NY, in the United States, after the war. Volume 1 was released in 1951, and by 1956, all 5 volumes of the collection were available to Russian Orthodox parishes. The liturgical material in the collection is distributed as follows:

Volume 1 (numbered in the edition as Part I):

a) Horologion, including the Sunday Epistle and Gospel readings from the Sunday of All Saints until the Sunday of the Publican and Pharisee, as well as the prokimena and Alleluia for Sundays and weekdays.

b) Sunday Ochtoechos

c) Resurrectional Exapostilaria and Gospel stichera

d) General Menaion.

Volume 2 (numbered in the edition as Part II, Book I): Festal Menaion: services for the great feasts of the Lord, the Theotokos, and great saints (September through February).

Volume 3 (numbered in the edition as Part II, Book II): Festal Menaion: services for the great feasts of the Lord, the Theotokos, and great saints (March through August).

Volume 4 (numbered in the edition as Part III): Lenten Triodion.

Volume 5 (numbered in the edition as Part III): the Flowery Triodion.

Thus, with these five books it became possible to carry out the accepted order of services on an émigré cliros for all Sundays and major feasts of the year. This is a great service of our monastic fathers in Jordanville. May their memory be eternal!

It is not surprising that the first part of this anthology, since it is most often used in the choir, comes into disrepair and needs repair or replacement faster than the others. As a result, this part of the collection at one time became a rarity. In recent years, a new printing was done in Europe with the agreement of Holy Trinity Monastery.

9. **Book of Needs** (Trebnik or Euchologion): This is another book required by any choir. In addition to public services—the Liturgy and All-night Vigil—there are also private services, requested by the faithful for personal reasons. These include baptisms, weddings, funerals, memorial services, and prayers for various needs. Precentors often have to sing at these services, and so they should be quite familiar with this book, and indeed with all the other books listed here.

For liturgical services in English we recommend the following:

Horologion – St.Tikhon's Seminary Press.

Unabbreviated Horologion or Book of Hours by Fr. Laurence Campbell, Jordanville.

Menaion – The St. John of Kronstadt Press.

Psalter – Holy Transfiguration Monastery Press.

Ochtoechos – The St. John of Kronstadt Press.

Apostol – St. Tikhon's Seminary Press.

The Book of Needs – 4 vol. set, St.Tikhon's Seminary Press.

Lenten Triodion – 2002, St. Tikhon's Seminary Press.

Lenten Triodion Supplementary Texts – 2007, St. Tikhon's Seminary Press.

Pentecostarion – The St. John of Kronstadt Press.

The mentioned texts include exclusively liturgical texts and do not contain any musical material.

§ 2
The Cliros Library – Anthologies of Sheet Music

In church practice, printed music books are referred to as *Obikhods*. Notated Obikhods may be divided into two categories:

1. Monophonic and

2. polyphonic.

Among monophonic Obikhods, the following should be mentioned firstly:

1. The ***Synodal Notated Obikhod*** in five parts, printed in square notation. It was repeatedly reprinted by the Synodal Press in Moscow and St. Petersburg between 1772 and 1913.

a) Part 1. All-night Vigil and Liturgy

b) Part 2. Ochtoecos.

c) Part 3. Feasts.

d) Part 4. Hirmologion.

e) Part 5. Triodion.

In the diaspora, a Uniate monastery in Belgium reprinted two parts: the All-night Vigil and Liturgy and the Triodion. In Russia, the Feasts collection was reprinted in 2002. Thus, the Octoechos and Hirmologion are still awaiting their republication.

2. The ***Precentor's Companion***, created in the early twentieth century as an outcome of the Precentors' congresses convened in Novgorod with the blessing of Archbishop Arseny (Stadnitsky). The collection is printed in square notation. The material is very convenient to use, which is especially evident during the period of Lent, when conducting weekday services.

The first few editions were printed before the 1917 revolution and were later reprinted by the Holy Trinity Monastery in Jordanville. As of 2019 they were still available for sale. The material in the *Precentor's Companion* can be thought of as a kind of distillation of the five-volume *Synodal Obikhod*, since this one book contains the music most needed by the choir for the liturgical year, selected from all five books of the *Synodal Obikhod*.

3. The **Obikhod of Liturgical Music of the Valaam Monastery**, published by the Valaam monastery in 1909. The monophonic melodies are written in the alto clef, which is the closest to the clef used in square notation. Until recently, this Obikhod could be purchased from the New Valamo Monastery in Finland.

4. The **Obikhod of the Solovki Monastery**, published by the Solovki monastery in 1912 and reprinted in Moscow by the "Life-Giving Spring" publishing house in 2004.

5. The **Monophonic Obikhod of the Great Assumption Cathedral of the Moscow Kremlin**. Reissued in Moscow by the "Life-Giving Spring" publishing house in 2005.

The above-mentioned five monophonic Obikhods are undoubtedly a valuable collection for any choir, especially for choirs where the singers are accustomed to the so-called "clerical harmonization" (as described by Gardner, and dealt with later in this textbook) and are able to sing in three or four voices from the monophonic Obikhod.

They should also be of particular interest to church composers and arrangers, since the melodic richness contained in these publications cannot be overstated. Particularly important in this respect is the *Solovki Obikhod*, which was never subjected to the ravages of the civil strife and the Tartar yoke in Russia, and, therefore, largely retained the features and spirit of the music of centuries past.

Polyphonic Obikhods are most often written for four voices, either for mixed or homogeneous choirs. Here, we will name a few of the most accessible editions.

1. The **Church Music Compendium**—an edition of the Educational Board of the Holy Synod in St. Petersburg, printed in in eight books (1902–1908). Reprinted by the Holy Trinity Monastery in Jordanville, NY (1970–1977) (eternal memory to its publisher, Archimandrite Anthony [Yamshchikov]). The reprint does not include the last part of the old edition—the Hirmologion.

The publication contains a lot of useful material, but because of its bulkiness, it is not widespread in choirs in the Russian Orthodox Church Outside of Russia. It is available in the bookshops at Holy Trinity Monastery.

2. The ***Court Obikhod*** of L'vov / Bakhmet'yev. Published by the Court Capella, it was used before the Russian Revolution in the parishes under the Department for Court Property and was widely criticized by zealots for the purity of native Russian church singing. Nonetheless, its use was quite common before the revolution. After the revolution, it was reissued in Poland; later, some parts were republished by the Department for the Eastern Rite at Fordham University. In the choirs of the Russian Orthodox Church Outside of Russia, they came to be known informally as the "Polish booklets." Certainly not the best option, but the emigrant community had to use what was at hand. Here and there, these little books still remain in use in ROCOR choirs to this day.

3. The ***Obikhod of Ledkovsky***, issued by Holy Trinity Monastery in 1958. It contains music for the All-night Vigil and resurrectional heirmoi from the Octoechos. It also includes some free compositions by Boris M. Ledkovsky (e.g., "Praise Ye the Name of the Lord").

This Obikhod, in contrast to the *Court Obikhod*, is written in a stricter style, using the Russian ecclesiastical mode, or scale. The more Western sound inherent in the *Court Obikhod* is absent from this Obikhod. The published Obikhod is labeled Part I; the second part was never published due to unclear circumstances. However, most of B. M. Ledkovsky's free compositions were published by Holy Trinity Monastery in subsequent years in the form of three separate collections (in 1959, 1972, and 1985), including approximately 85 works.

4. We draw the reader's particular attention to the musical collections published by the Trinity St. Sergius Lavra, edited by the ever-memorable Archimandrite Matthew (Mormyl'). These include: the *All-Night Vigil* (2000), *Divine Liturgy* (2009), *Music of Passion Week* (2000), *Music of the Lenten Triodion* (2000), the *Service of the Passion of Christ* (1997), *Automela of Ancient Monastic Usage* (1999), and the *Acathist to the Sweetest Jesus* (1999).

5. **The *Anthology of Russian Orthodox Liturgical Music*,** 2 volumes (1962), the so-called *London Compendia*. These anthologies received this name because they were published with grants from the heterodox College of Faith in London and printed in England. The editorial board responsible for these collections was mainly based in Paris, with most of its members based at the St. Sergius Podvorie and its related theological institute.

The collections contain valuable music material in two volumes: volume 1, Music for the Divine Liturgy (1962), and volume 2 – Music for the Fixed Portions of the All-Night Vigil (1975). Unfortunately, despite the high typographical quality, the London anthologies contain numerous errors in the notation. Therefore, anyone using them should do so with care.

When it comes to printed music in Church Slavonic, there is no longer that acute a shortage as was experienced even twenty to twenty-five years ago. After the Perestroika and subsequent changes in Russia, many religious publishers emerged, and they have not neglected the needs of church singers.

Today, one may find anthologies of sacred music in Church Slavonic of varies categories. For example, if in the past we were accustomed to seeing only collections with titles like "All-Night Vigil," "Divine Liturgy," "Pannychida," and so on, it is now possible to find collections of a narrower focus, with titles like: "Automela," "Prokimena," "Cherubic Hymns," "Hymns of Ascents in the Eight Tones," and so forth. This development is most welcome.

In addition to collections released by publishing houses in major Russian cities, there are provincial (mostly diocesan) musical publications, which are also of interest. However, we recommend exercising care in selecting from such material for use in your parish, since among works of high musical quality one can sometimes encounter quite mediocre compositions.

In addition to printed editions of church music both in Russia and abroad, relatively recently a separate layer of such publications has appeared in electronic format (see appendix 11). The ever-memorable Alexander B. Ledkovsky (d. 2004) labored in this field. For five years—from 1999 to the end of 2004—he published a large volume of music for (mostly) movable hymns on the Internet, for example preparing the music for Troparia and Kontakia for the coming Sunday or holiday. This site is still in existence and the material is available to those who need it at http://www.rocm.org.

We should also mention here the US publishing house, Musica Russica. It began with an idea to publish an anthology of stellar examples of Russian liturgical music in conjunction with the commemoration of the Millenium of the Baptism of Rus in 1988. The project resulted in a wide-ranging, heavy folio, comprising compositions of various eras and styles heard in the Russian church throughout the first thousand years of its existence. The sponsor of this project was the Russian patriotic youth organization the National Organization of Russian Scouts (NORR), which wanted to contribute in a significant way to the general mission of the Russian emigration to commemorate the millennium of the baptism.

After the festivities, the project was taken over by Vladimir P. Morozan, who with some success issued subsequent volumes, which thus turned into a series, on the principle of a volume per composer. Thus we now have volumes that contain the full sacred works of Titov, Rachmaninoff, Tchaikovsky, Rimsky-Korsakov. These may have value for English-speaking singers singing in Slavonic, because the Slavonic text in these volumes is given in transliteration.

Over the past decades, our church membership has changed significantly in demographic terms. This is naturally reflected in our work in church choirs. The main issue we face in this regard is the issue of the liturgical language. The Church Abroad bears its ministry not only in English-speaking North America and Australia; our parishes in the non-English speaking diaspora countries often serve in the local language as well. Linguistic assimilation is a challenge to some extent faced by all and there is no cookie-cutter solution.

For example, even before the revolution of 1917, texts were translated into German on the initiative of the Berlin archpriest A. P. Maltsev (1856–1915). Touching on the local situation in the United States, the future Patriarch Tikhon, who was at the time the ruling archbishop in North America, blessed some translations by Mrs. Isabel Hapgood (1851–1928), an Anglican who never did convert to Orthodoxy. The first translation, under the title *Service Book of the Holy Orthodox-Catholic (Greco-Russian) Church*, appeared in 1906, followed by the second in 1922. Later, this book was republished numerous times by the North American archdiocese of the Antiochian Patriarchate.

In the Far East, this question is treated idiosyncratically. In Japan, one finds to this day that the *Court Obikhod* is in wide use, as are the compositions of Bortniansky. This is not surprising, if we consider that the Apostol to Japan St. Nicholas's liturgical cultural background was steeped in St. Petersburg. In China, today, a Chinese female composer is writing liturgical music, which reflects the folk character of Chinese music, based on the pentatonic scale and at the same time is extremely prayerful, as we were able to ascertain during a visit to church services in Hong Kong.

Coming back to the situation in the United States, we should note that there are ongoing efforts to translate liturgical books into English. For example, at the Synod of Bishops in New York, the Synodal translator Brother Isaac Lambertsen worked for many years, up until his death in 2017 (just prior to his repose he was tonsured a monk, under the name of Joseph). Of his many works, special mention goes to the *Menaion* (in 12 volumes) and a number of other valuable translations. St. Vladimir's Seminary Press (Orthodox Church in America) has also published a number of valuable liturgical books in English. They have also published a multivolume collection of liturgical music in English, which includes numerous harmonizations by B. M. Ledkovsky, who served for many years at St. Vladimir's Seminary teaching liturgical music.

§ 3
Reading on the Cliros

The reading of liturgical texts on the cliros is one of the most important elements of Orthodox worship, no less important than singing itself. This is evident from the fact that the first order of the clergy is called the "order of the reader and singer." The fact that people are elected to these orders from the body of the laity indicates the importance of this liturgical function. During their election, readers are blessed to wear the sticharion, the liturgical vestment that is proper to their order. Thus, in times past only men could carry out this function; they were considered minor clergy ("d'yachki"). The exception was convents, where all functions on the cliros were carried out by nuns. In our time, in practice, reading on the cliros by women is blessed as well, but without a blessing to wear the sticharion. (As for liturgical singing, women began to participate in church choirs in Russia at the end of the nineteenth century).

As in singing, the chief task of church readers is to proclaim the liturgical text so that it edifies the conscience and heart of the congregants. For this reason, their reading must meet the following criteria:

1. It must be loud enough, so that it can be heard in all locations of the church building, but not too loud so as to sound like shouting.

2. It must be understandable and delivered with good diction, at a measured pace. The reader should not "swallow" individual syllables, or even sometimes whole words. Unfortunately, we often find abuses in the practice of reading on cliros. The most obvious is reading too fast. Some readers even demonstrably boast about the speed of their reading. (For example, at a certain seminary students would use a sports chronometer in a contest to see who could set the record speed in the reading of morning and evening prayers). This problem becomes particularly acute during the reading of the Six Psalms, which some read at lightning speed, without paying any attention to the meaning of the words. Another common problem is rushing through the reading of "Lord, have mercy" forty times (Slavonic: "Gospodi, pomiluy"), which in Slavonic in particular begins to sound like a mantra "pimkhos, pimkhos, pimkhos, pimkhos." On the other hand, one should not fall into the opposite extreme and artificially drag out the reading, either.

3. It must be free from passion. Texts should be read in an emotionally neutral (but not mechanistic) fashion. Evenness in reading helps each congregant perceive it in accordance with his individual internal state and take from it that which is most spiritually useful to him at that moment. The emotional reader conveys an impression of spiritual delusion (*prelest'*), to the consternation of the listener. The reader should not impose his own emotions on the listeners as they may be alien to the inner mood of the worshipers. In emotional reading, the reader often risks falling into the trap of "theatricality," which sounds

completely out of place and vulgar in the general context of the service.

4. It must be meaningful. The reader must understand the content of the text that he is reading; if he does so, his listeners will also understand it better. Therefore, it is always useful to get acquainted with the liturgical texts before an important feast, especially if the reader does not have much experience in this matter. It is necessary to pay special attention to the syntax, so that the reader's phrasing does not contradict the meaning of what is being read.

5. It must agree with the rules of the language. In modern (twenty-first-century) conditions, in many churches outside of Russia the services are conducted in the language of the country of residence. While the above four recommendations apply to reading in any liturgical language, it is up to the rector to involve persons sufficiently literate in the local language to conduct worship services. At the same time, there are quite a few churches outside of Russia where the liturgical Church Slavonic language is still widely used. It functions as the common linking factor in the liturgical life of the diaspora, just as not so long ago the Latin language that was obligatory in the Roman Catholic Church was a strong link for world Catholicism. In those parishes where Church Slavonic continues to be used (even if it is not used as the main liturgical language) readers should pay attention to the phonetic rules of this language. Because of its many similarities to Russian, the most common and obvious mistake occurs when readers pronounce Church Slavonic as they would Russian. Here are just a few of the most basic differences:

a) In the Church Slavonic language there is no "Moscow-style use of 'a'" ("akan'ye"). All occurrences of "o" are pronounced as "o," regardless of whether they are stressed or not. Therefore, it is really unpleasant for the ear to hear, for example, the pronunciation of the opening of the 50th psalm as "P**a**miluy, mya Bozhe, p**a** velitsey mil**a**sti Tv**a**yey," etc.

b) The sound "yo" is also absent from Church Slavonic. In those cases where the Russian word has the sound "yo," the letter "ye" will always be pronounced in Church Slavonic as "ye." For example, "tvo**ye**" and not "tvo**yo**," "mo**ye**" and not "mo**yo**," "tv**ye**rdy" and not "tv**yo**rdy," etc.

c) The plosive Russian sound "g" in Church Slavonic is pronounced softly, somewhere between "g" and "h." At the same time, this sound should not be pronounced completely like a fricative, as is typical in the Ukrainian "**H**ospodi pomiluy" or "Bo**h**oroditse," etc.

In addition, Church Slavonic uses many diacritical marks, mainly accents (which sometimes make reading much easier), and all kinds of "titlo" (abbreviation marks) denoting omitted letters. There is also a number of letters that do not coincide with the modern Russian alphabet. These are either of Greek origin or are archaic Slavic letters. All this, and much more, is found in our liturgical books, and therefore readers in churches of the Russian Orthodox Church where services are conducted in Church Slavonic have the duty to become familiar with the rules of the language to the extent they need for successful and competent work on the cliros.

§ 4
Kievan Square Notation

Commonly Used Symbols of Kievan Square Notation

Symbol	Name	Description
♦	Whole note (long note)	The effective pitch is located at the intersection of the two diamonds.
⊣	Half note (moderate note)	
⌐	Quarter note (fast note)	
⌐̧	Eighth note (very fast note)	Used on the middle line of the staff and above. The effective pitch is on the upper diamond.
ʯ	Eighth note (very fast note)	Used below the middle line of the staff.

ᗡ	**Tse-fa-ut clef**	The C-clef in square notation. The square head is always on the middle line.
ᗢ	**Final note**	The effective pitch is located between the two rectangles. The equivalent of a note with a fermata.
♭	**Flat sign**	Indicates that a note is lowered by a half step. Used only on the seventh ascending degree of the scale.
∫	**End of piece sign**	Printed at the end of a piece of hymnography.
▭	**Recitative mark**	Indicates recitative on one note for an extended period.
◆	**Augmentation dot**	Increases the length of a note by one and a half times (just as in round notation)

The ability to sight read Kievan square notation is an absolutely necessary skill for any church singer, and even more so for the choir director. Nonetheless, not all directors possess this skill. Even many musically literate singers on cliros feel unsure of themselves when they open the Obikhod in square notation. Our task, then, is to uproot the widely spread phobia regarding the use of this notation. Here, it is pertinent to recall the Psalmist David, who wrote, "There were they in great fear, where no fear was" (Ps. 52:6), in other words, there is no reason to be afraid.

Indeed, we hear those who claim that square notation has already outlived its usefulness, and that it's time to switch completely over to round notation, so that everyone will feel comfortable. However, we will note that when everyone is comfortable, life becomes a lot less interesting. That is the first consideration. The second is that no one will argue with the fact that square notation is conducive to greater expressivity than round notation, given its elasticity, that is, the absence of the sense of "metronome" that characterizes and therefore constricts round notation, where two quarter notes must always equal one half note, etc. This elasticity of square notation allows the Word to dominate over the Note, and to more effectively transmit the meaning of the text. Third, familiarity with square notation will help those competent musicians who, knowing only round notation, have a panic attack when the choir director on cliros opens up the *Church Singer's Companion*. Fourth, singing from round notation is also somewhat uncomfortable because when singing from it one always has the sense that the notes on the page should correspond exactly to the indicated pitch, which is not the case in square notation, and which causes extreme difficulties for those with "absolute pitch," who cannot hear an F# on the written (round note) page as anything other than an F#, a difficulty that disappears with square notation.

Moreover, it should be noted that square notation has much in common with the round notation familiar to most singers, and is even simpler in some ways. The origin of this notation is also Western European; it came to Russia at the end of the seventeenth century, when it was brought, together with the Kievan Chant, from the southwestern lands.

As mentioned above, the Obikhod books written in this notation contain a rich, almost inexhaustible, melodic repertoire, very useful for the composer and arranger of church music. These books served as a source of inspiration for such talented musicians as Sergei Rachmaninov, Pyotr Tchaikovsky, Pavel Chesnokov, Aleksandr Kastalsky, and others. They did not want to write church music in the Western style, but, on the contrary, highly prized their national musical heritage, and turned to it for creative inspiration.

**Common characteristics
of round and square notations:**

1. Both are written on the five-lined staff.

2. The pitch is indicated by notes, which have a head and stem, placed on a staff.

3. In both notations, the notes have varying duration.

4. In both notations, the augmentation dot is used to extend the duration by 1.5 times.

5. In both notations, a clef is placed at the beginning of the staff.

It must be remembered that square notation is considerably easier to use than round notation. This is demonstrated by the following characteristics:

Differences between square and round notation:

1. Unlike round notation, where each staff has either a treble clef or a bass clef (rarely – an alto clef or a tenor clef), square notation uses only one clef: ⌐, called the tse-fa-ut clef, which indicates the placement of the tonic on the middle line of the staff. In this way, the tse-fa-ut clef is like the alto clef.

2. Square notation does not use accidentals (sharps, flats, and naturals) and does not use key signatures after the clef, as in round notation. The only exception is the flat sign –♭–, which is written on the seventh ascending degree of the Obikhod scale to preserve its modality.

3. Square notation does not indicate the key of a piece (e.g., d-minor, F-major, and so on). In this way, it does not indicate the absolute starting pitch of a piece. Rather, the singer can choose whatever pitch is convenient for his or her vocal range. Along those same lines, in polyphonic, i.e., choral performance, the choir director chooses the tonality that is the most comfortable with respect to the voices present in the given choral ensemble.

4. Square notation lacks a time signature that indicates the metrical structure of a piece. Proper measure bar lines are also absent. The bar lines placed in square notation are not based on beats in a measure, but rather on the phrasing of the text.

5. Square notation lacks indications of dynamics and tempo, for example, *forte, piano, adagio, allegro*.

Since in the Russian Orthodox Church square notation replaced the Znamenny neumatic ("hook") notation that came before it, the following things should be kept in mind when singing chant recorded in square notation:

1. Znamenny notation, being strictly vocal, contains many nuances and peculiarities of performance technique, which cannot be

adequately captured by square notation. This specifically concerns things like intonation and rhythmic accents.

2. Since words are most important in Orthodox hymnography, it is the words of the hymnography that determine the various nuances and rhythmic accents, rather than the notation.

3. For this reason professor Ivan Gardner reminds us that the metronomic accuracy and rhythmical tightness of Western European music—which limits the expressive nature of the performance—is not appropriate in the performance of liturgical music. The exception in Western music is Gregorian chant (which, in any case, is an Orthodox, pre-Schism chant). Gardner in fact calls it the cousin to Znamenny.

4. The length of notes in round notation has a strict 2:1 relationship; that is, there are two half notes in a whole note; two quarter notes in a half note; two eighth notes in a quarter note, and so forth. In square notation, these relationships are more elastic. Though we speak of square notes as having equivalents in round notation, i.e., we call them a) whole ♪, b) ♩ half, c) ♩ quarter, d) ♪ ♪ eighth, (notes of shorter duration do not exist in square notation), it is more appropriate to think of them as a) long, b) moderate, c) fast, and d) very fast.

5. Again Ivan Gardner, citing authoritative chant masters of the seventeenth century, recommends that when square notes are transcribed to round notation, the long note is rendered not as a whole note, but as a half note; the moderate note not as a half note, but as a quarter note; the fast note not as a quarter note, but as an eighth note. With this relationship, "all melodies recorded in square notation receive a certain swiftness; their viscosity goes away. This is a purely psychological phenomenon: a piece recorded in round half notes is automatically performed slower than a piece recorded in quarter notes."[1]

It is appropriate to mention here one more archaic facet of our cliros practice, which sometimes may still be encountered today. We refer now

---

[1] I. A. Gardner, "O Sinodal'nyh bogosluzhebnyh pevcheskikh knigakh i o penii po nim," *Pravoslavny Put'*, Jordanville, NY, 1971.

not to square notation, but to the notated books published in the nineteenth century, for example, the *Obikhod* published by Bakhmetev in 1868 in St. Petersburg (see appendix 1). It is printed not in the usual treble clef, but in the C-clef: 𝄡. The bass part uses the normal bass clef.

This clef has the same shape as the alto clef, consisting of two semicircles; however, it moves up or down at the beginning of the staff, depending on which voice (soprano, alto, or tenor) is singing the music in this staff. The purpose of this clef is to show the relative pitch of the music in this staff by indicating the position of C and eliminating the need for additional ledger lines.

The position of this C is determined by the line located between the two semicircles. Thus in the soprano part, the semicircles surround the first (i.e., lower) line of the staff; in the alto – the third (i.e. middle) line; and in the tenor – the fourth (i.e., the second from the top) line (see appendix 2).

The purpose of this arrangement is to ensure that the main tessitura of the voices fits as much as possible within the lines of the staff so that there would be no need to use ledger lines. Nowadays the use of such an arrangement is seen as obsolete and has fallen into disuse, not in the least because playing such choral scores, recorded in different keys, on the piano is overly complicated. (In addition to full scores, separated notation books for each vocal part were also published; these may still occasionally be encountered in our choirs). It should be noted that it is actually not difficult to sing from such notation; the important thing here is that the choir director know how to give the pitch in this situation. These archaeological relics occasionally show up in the cupboards of our choir lofts.

§ 5
Singing to the Tonal Melodies

Our liturgical singing is based on a system of the eight tones, called the "Octoechos." This system is the foundation of the entire Christian singing tradition, both Eastern and Western. This tradition originated in many centuries ago.

Its beginning dates back to the seventh century, and it appeared in the Byzantine Empire and spread to Georgia, Armenia, Syria, Egypt,

Romania, and the Slavic countries. In the West, it appeared in the form of Gregorian Chant in the Roman Catholic Church and the Anglican tradition. Not limited to our usual major-minor sound, it had a modal character and each of the eight tones represented its own special scale. A close connection with the Byzantine tradition also appears to have existed in medieval Russia and it appears that early on the "Russian" eight tones followed the model of the Byzantine modes. However, in the Russian case, under the influence of Western European secular music, over time, the modal eight tone system gave way to a set of major-minor melodies, which, embodied in the notorious *Obikhod* of Lvov, was promoted by Emperor Nicholas I himself (no more, no less) but was rejected and banned by Metropolitan Philaret (Drozdov; †1867) within his Moscow diocese. Bakhmetev's *Obikhod* is not much different qualitatively from Lvov's. Until recently, both the L'vov and Bakhmetev Obikhods were widely used in our churches. Some antidote to this unfortunate situation was provided by the late Boris Ledkovsky with his *Obikhod*, in which he adhered to the Russian modal scale in harmonizations. This *Obikhod*, despite its age (1958) and limited circulation, still may be found, both in Russia and abroad. This is to be welcomed. Here we should note the positive influence of émigré ecclesiastical centers, such as the Holy Trinity Monastery in North America and the Paris St.-Sergius Podvorie in Europe in the task of eliminating, or rather, replacing the "Polish booklets," although these latter did serve a useful purpose at a time when nothing else was available). So many people visit these centers, where they are able to hear properly executed Obikhod singing and even to sing in the monastery choir. They bring this tradition back to their own churches, significantly improving Obikhod singing at the parish level.

In general, it should be said that in the matter of church singing, both Western and Eastern, two positions coexist in a peculiar way. On the one hand, there are canonical prohibitions on composed works, with instructions to adhere to monastic chants. (The 7th Ecumenical Council and the Council in Trullo dealt with these issues.) On the other hand, we have established practice, which basically "does not notice" these prohibitions, or rather, does not pay the slightest attention to them. It should be noted that the ecclesiastical authorities look at this issue with considerable leniency. As for composed works, we see one of two things: either the composition does not correspond to the content of the text and the spirit of Orthodox liturgy, or the composer has managed to find the necessary liturgical character. In the latter case, the highest praise for the composer occurs when his work takes on some anonymity and his name is replaced by the adjective "Obikhod." The most striking example of this is the "Feofanovsky" "Mercy of Peace" as well as the eponymous Doxology, which are universally considered to be "Obikhod," even though Feofan was an archimandrite and rector of the Donskoy Monastery in Moscow. The same can be said about some of Bortnyansky's works, which have become so ingrained in the flesh and blood of our singing that they are perceived as "Obikhod." These include our simplest "Many Years," the "Ispolla" trio, "Beneath your compassion", the hirmoi of the Great Canon, "Come Let Us Bless Joseph," and a number of other compositions. There are other composers who have received this honor.

The leader of the choir needs to master the eight tones to perfection. What does this mean, practically? We have eight tones, and five liturgical types of hymns: troparia, stichera, the verses to the stichera, hirmoi, prokeimena. Therefore, since any of them can turn up during the service at any time, you need to memorize (like a multiplication table) at least forty melodies in order to adequately conduct any ordinary service. In addition, it is recommended to familiarize yourself with a special category of chants called the "podoben" (automela). These are varieties of melodies within a given tone, and it is not necessary to perform them, since you can simply sing according to the indicated tone. However, their competent execution will qualitatively raise the level of your service by several orders of magnitude. There is no point in studying all the automela, because there are a lot of them (more than 480), and some of them are used quite rarely. It is enough to learn a dozen of the most common ones, and your service will literally "come to life." Some of the most common automela have been printed in a separate brochure in an arrangement by Archimandrite Matthew by the Holy Trinity-St. Sergius Lavra.

So, the choir director-precentor faces a monumental, but blessed task. There is no need to be afraid of it, for the following reasons:

1. Let us recall the proverb, "Fear has great eyes," and the above mentioned observation of King David, "There were they in great fear, where no fear was" (Ps. 52:6).
2. If you regularly attend church (especially the All-Night Vigil), many of these melodies are already well known to you. You just need to figure out what you already know and what you don't know yet, and sort it out in your mind.
3. Cross-check your knowledge with the "cheat sheet" offered in appendix 4, or make your own according to this same model and start with the material you know, then proceeding to the unfamiliar material. Some categories of chants are repeated (for example, in the fifth tone, troparia, stichera, and hirmoi can be sung to the same melody. In the third tone, stichera and hirmoi also coincide).

A Note about the Podobny

The "podobny" (automela) exist in all of the tones and are identified by the initial words of the automelon. Here, we list the most common, so to speak "most popular," ones:

1. Tone 1: "Joy of the Ranks of Heaven," "O wonderous marvel"

2. Tone 2: "Down from the tree," "House of Ephratha"

3. Tone 4: "As one valiant among the martyrs," "Called from on high," "Though hast given a sign"

4. Tone 5: "Rejoice, life-giving cross"

5. Tone 6: "Thou didst rise from the tomb," "Having placed all their hope"

6. Tone 8: "O all-glorious wonder"

Learn at least these podobny (see appendix 5), and you will feel a "new life" in your churches.

The melodic examples for tonal singing given in the musical appendix (appendix 6) are selected according to the practice of the Holy Trinity Monastery in Jordanville and its associated seminary, because this is the training house for parish priests in ROCOR and these melodies, with rare exceptions, are used everywhere in our church. It is absolutely necessary for the leader of the choir to know them.

How to Use the Cheat Sheet:

There is no one correct answer to this question, because the degree of "churchness" and musical training is different for everyone. Everyone knows these melodies to one degree or another by ear (depending on their church attendance), though that knowledge is often very fragmented. A person may know "O heavenly King," but he most likely does not realize that this can serve as a model for singing stichera in Tone 6. Or he knows "Save, O Lord, Thy people" or "Thy Nativity, Christ Our God," but he is unaware that the troparia of the first and fourth tones should also be sung in this way. Therefore, you need to put in the work, and having ascertained the level of your own knowledge, make yourself a cheat sheet according to the model offered here (appendix r). Since the troparia of the Great Feasts are easier to remember even than the Sunday ones, in the proposed scheme we give troparion tones according to the troparia of the Great Feasts that coincide with them. We give some other familiar melodies for the stichera tones. As for hirmoi and prokeimena, they simply need to be learned. When you find familiar melodies, write down their names in your cheat sheet. To memorize the stichera tones, seminary students are required to memorize all eight resurrectional dogmatic theotokia, which is not so difficult, since the melody is learned more easily in combination with the text. For students initially with zero knowledge, we suggest mastering the material in appendix 3.

A Comment on the Various "Raspevy"/Chants in the Liturgical Practice of the Russian Orthodox Church

This topic is very confusing, due to the social changes introduced by Peter I into the life of the Russian Empire in the late seventeenth/early eighteenth century. It is customary for us to use the term "raspev" ("chant") for a corpus of melodies, generalized by specific characteristics, melodic or rhythmic. The tradition of the Russian Orthodox Church knows the Znamenny, Kievan, Greek (in great and small varieties), and also Bulgarian chants. The only true chant, by definition, is the most ancient, Znamenny, since you cannot confuse it with anything, given its characteristic melodic formulas and syncopations. As for the rest, according to A. Preobrazhensky, they appeared in Muscovite Russia in the seventeenth century, brought there by Kievan singers, who were patronized by Tsar Alexey Mikhailovich and Patriarch Nikon. Given such patronage, their rapid spread is unsurprising.

The Znamenny chant apparently remained in use among the Old Believers, who were in opposition to the tsar and the patriarch. Moreover, the monophonic Znamenny chant was never banned in the "official" Church but simply gradually fell out of general use; it was preserved in places, for example, in the Dormition Cathedral of the Moscow Kremlin, revered as the cathedral of "All Rus'." The same Preobrazhensky points out that the Bulgarian and Greek chant came into the Russian tradition thanks to the contacts of the Kievan monks with the Athos monasteries. And the Muscovites of that time apparently adapted these chants in their own way so that both the Greeks and the Bulgarians no longer recognize the melodies attributed to them. Musically, they differ little from each other and their "genealogy," so to speak, is very unclear. So from all these melodies of chants over the past three centuries, such a hybrid has emerged that it's hard to say for sure what is what. It would be more accurate to conditionally define them as "the so-called Greek, or Kievan or Bulgarian chants." And here the matter is further complicated by the presence also of different variants, which we will call the chants of monastic origin: the Kiev Caves (which is different from Kievan), Valaam, Holy Trinity-St. Sergius Lavra, Optina Hermitage, Glinsky Hermitage, and many others. In addition, in monasteries there exist systems of chant melodies proper to each individual monastery. All of this is enough to make a cliros neophyte's head spin.

About Differences in Melodies within the Same Tone

Sometimes there are apparent contradictions in the performance of one tone or another. One should not be perplexed by this, because our church musical heritage contains a great variety of different chants and melodies: Znamenny, Greek, Kievan, Bulgarian, and all of them are present in our cliros practice today, and figuratively speaking, represent a kind of curious Russian salad on our liturgical menu. Let us briefly present some observations, at least regarding the troparion melodies.

1. Tone 1: Everything is clear, there are no discrepancies in performance practice.

2. Tone 2: Here there is an "argument" between the melodies for stichera (abbreviated Kievan chant) and troparia (abbreviated Greek chant). The troparia are sometimes sung to the stichera tone (the reverse does not happen).
3. Tone 3: Here the interchange happens between the melodies of the stichera and hirmoi.
4. Tone 4: We have a choice between:

a. The simplest version (as in "Theotokos, Virgin rejoice."

b. The Greek chant as harmonized by M. S. Konstantinov.

c. The harmonization of B. M. Ledkovsky.

d. The Moscow version as harmonized by Kastalsky.

5. Tone 5: troparia, stichera, and hirmoi may be sung to the same tune. Hirmoi are sometimes also sung in the abridged Znamenny chant. We recommend that the harmonization of Ledkovsky's *Obikhod* for stichera at "Lord, I have cried" be applied to the troparia as well. It is well worth it.

6. Tone 6: No discrepancies. Here everything is clear.

7. Tone 7: Usually in the diaspora, the abridged Bulgarian chant is performed. In Moscow, there has arisen its own tradition also in the Bulgarian chant, but in its own local variant.

8. Tone 8: the "universal" 8th tone melody that we have is abridged Kievan chant and is quite banal in its sound. In its usual performance it resembles the sound of a hurdy-gurdy. Just turn the knob and get the eighth tone. This melody is flawed not only because it resembles a hurdy-gurdy, which one could endure. Things are worse here, because in some cases, the text itself is distorted through incorrect transfer of stress, particularly in the Church Slavonic. For example: "славнейшую" instead of "сла́внейшую," "без истления" instead of "без истле́ния," "благодарстве́нная" instead of "благода́рственная," etc. Fortunately, we have a worthy alternative, namely a melody in the same tone, also called the Kievan Chant, but apparently not abridged. Here we do not find the ad nauseum repetition of four notes, eternally moving up and down the scale. It is also very convenient to sing "It is

truly meet" on melodies other than the designated troparia tone 8. The most popular versions here are stichera tones 3 and 7, and hirmoi tone 8, and also some podobny: the text comfortably fits with the melodies of several, such as "Joy of the Ranks of Heaven" (see appendix 7). For example, a truly memorable setting of this text may be heard at the Trinity-St. Sergius Lavra, to the melody of "By the wave of the sea," in the harmonization of Father Matthew Mormyl, even though this melody does not belong to the generally accepted corpus of podobny. It should also be noted that this same melody is used in some English-language funerals, and sounds quite nice. The Slavonic text of the hirmoi "As Israel traversed the sea" also fits quite well with the melody to "By the waves of the sea." Here there is food for thought.

In general, the late Father Matthew was a great master of transposing familiar everyday chants to the most unexpected, but yet familiar melodies of other chants. (For example, "From my youth" in the likeness of "In Thy Kingdom" of the Moscow melody). One can only rejoice at such elasticity of choral creativity, because this testifies to a lively attitude to the matter, instead of the often encountered rigidity and narrow-mindedness. However, such creativity requires a certain amount of literacy, so as not to fall into an absurd situation. I recall a tragicomic incident when one choir director sang the Paschal hirmoi as a catabasia at the beginning of Great Lent, motivating this by the fact that the hirmoi of other feasts (Exaltation, Nativity, Hypapante) are sung in anticipation of their feast so as to prepare us. Hence, why not to sing them before the "feast of feasts"? He had one irresistible argument to all objections: "No, no, you don't tell me that it's wrong, I graduated from the Music School in Jordanville." An ironclad argument, to be sure.

§ 6
"Clerical Harmonization"

The famous church musicologist Ivan Alekseyevich Gardner provides the following information about the origin of this type of singing. "Although all of the melodies in the Synodal music books are recorded for one voice (i.e., only the melody is provided), from the middle of the seventeenth century, probably under the influence of singers from Kiev accustomed to polyphonic, rather than unison, singing, the practice of singing from the Synodal musical books in two, three, and even four voices emerged. The main melody is sung by the second voice; the first (upper) voice goes in parallel with it a third higher (less often, it is done the other way around: the first voice sings according to the notes printed in the music books, the second accompanies it a third below; this is how, for example, the Great Doxology in Little Znamenny Chant is performed); the bass picks up by ear the fundamental tones of the chords outlined by the upper voices. If there is one more voice (baritone), then it complements the missing note of the chords. This method of improvised harmonization of the main melody is called "d'yachkovskaya garmonizatsiya" ("clerical harmonization"); in the previous (nineteenth) century and at the beginning of our (twentieth) century, minor clergy in Moscow were especially famous for this style of singing. In the same way, the signers sang from the Synodal music books in many monasteries and even in parish churches at weekday services."[2]

Thus, we see that this kind of harmonization developed in those churches where it was not possible to perform complex *partes* compositions, that is, in such monasteries and parish churches where, most often, minor clergy or monks sang on the cliros, rather than professional singers. This suggests that it is this type of singing, which is organically connected with what can be considered Obikhod, that is, those chants directly related to the liturgical cycles—the two Triodia, the Menaion, the Octoechos—that forms the true core of liturgical singing. Here we have an obvious case of improvisational art, which requires certain experience, skills, and literacy, both musical and general. In our time, certain monasteries in Russia and Ukraine, first of all the Holy Trinity St. Sergius Lavra, serve as the highest standard of this kind of singing. One can see this when visiting the weekday religious services there, and also certainly at the Kievo-Pechersk Lavra with its rich melodic heritage, which is beautifully performed there to this day. It is clear to those present at these services that it is precisely such singing that touches the believing soul much deeper than various composers' gimmicks. This once again confirms

---

[2] I. A. Gardner, preface to *Obikhod Notnogo Peniia*, Chevtogne, Belgium, 1966.

the greater significance and relevance of Obikhod singing, rather than *partes*, in the church.

Based on the cliros experience of our time, it is possible to point out some features of the use of clerical harmonization. Thus, given the completely natural parallel movement of the two upper voices, the movement of the lower voices parallel to them is highly undesirable. Singing the chant melody by the bass an octave lower should also be avoided. Singers who are improvising the bass line should move in a contrasting motion, if possible: when the upper voices move up, the bass should move down, and vice versa. Where this is not possible, then while moving in the same direction, movement in parallel fifths or octaves should be avoided. However, it should be noted that there is historical evidence that monks and clergy in the past centuries often sang not at all according to the rules of German harmony, which have affected modern practice, but in parallel fifths and octaves. In this there was a special archaic beauty, which was noticed by the composers of the Moscow School.

What should be the voice leading in this style of singing? As for the top two voices, they are only expected to sing the specified melody exactly. In their case, improvisation is absent, only the specified melodic contours need to be performed cleanly.

Improvisation concerns the bottom two voices. They are required to have even more musical sensitivity, a kind of cliros instinct, than the top voices, since their part is not recorded in the music. We have already discussed the bass voice leading. Here, it should also be remembered that it is this vocal part that gives the general harmonic direction to the music. As for the fourth voice (baritone), its task is to ensure the completeness of the chord. The baritone must sing softly, not annoyingly, and, in any case, should never stand out. Often the baritone part must merge with the bass, or with the second tenor, temporarily losing its independent sound. It is usually the case that the baritone sings in a very narrow tessitura, smoothly moving between 2, 3, or 4 notes, which requires the highest level of musical sensitivity, much greater than that of the three other voices.

So, in clerical harmonization, the voices are distributed in this way:

	male	female	mixed	(without tenor) small mixed
third above	1st tenor	1st soprano	tenor	soprano
melody	2nd tenor	2nd soprano	soprano	alto
filler	baritone	1st alto	alto	------
harm. foundation	bass	2nd alto	bass	bass

We give preference to this distribution of voices due to their specific timbre qualities. The soprano, because it has the highest vocal frequencies, has a tendency toward a certain fragility of sound, particularly on the higher notes, which frequently turns into a rattle or a tremolo, which elicits an undesirable agitated mood in church singing. The tenor sounds "calmer," and for that reason, in the question of who should sing the upper third we give that voice preference. This of course is a subjective viewpoint, especially if the tenor and soprano are of equal quality in a particular choir. The assessment of the quality of the voices and their distribution is of course the prerogative of the choir director. We provide here a few additional perfectly acceptable schema:

	Mixed	Small mixed (without alto)	or
Third above	soprano	tenor	soprano
Main melody	alto	soprano	tenor
Filler	tenor	---------	--------
harm. foundation	bass	bass	bass

To a beginner, singing in four voices from monophonic square notation can seem to be quite complicated, because it requires a certain skill and musical instinct and is a type of improvisational art.

However, there is another kind of cliros singing that requires even more musical skill than the above case. Here we are talking about singing in four voices without any musical notation at all, according to a book where only the liturgical text with an indication of a tone or melody ("podoben"/automelon) is given, as is often the case with our choirs. This is truly the highest class of choir singing. This type of improvisational art requires a certain level of auditory and vocal skills, as well as a general liturgical culture and familiarity with the grammar and syntax of the liturgical language. (In our case, Church Slavonic, or the local national language). In addition, it requires a thorough knowledge of the system of eight tones, which is the foundation of liturgical singing in general. More than that, those singing from the text of the liturgical books without notation should know how to combine the musical phrases with the phrases of the performed text, so that they sound meaningful and organic. If the phrases are not marked out in advance, then it is the rare cliros leader/choir director who can accomplish this task impromptu. And it is truly wonderful to see such a virtuoso at work when the opportunity arises.

With this style of singing, the choir director (unless he or she is a virtuoso) should preview the liturgical text in advance and (using a pencil so as not to destroy the book with ink) mark out the phrases so that those in the congregation can easily understand the meaning of what they hear (for alas, not all of us are virtuosi).

§ 7
About Singing Recitative

Here we will touch on yet another facet of kliros practice, namely the so-called *chitok* (recitative). We do not promote this practice as an absolutely necessary one, and don't recommend engaging in it without substantial preparation/training. In many of our churches this practice is completely unknown, and so no one will demand it from you. It is not at all shameful to sing without it. But if it is performed well, at a decent level, the perception of worship is given some additional dimension, which is difficult to convey in words. It affects the emotional side of the listener with its dynamism, as well as the rational one, clearly conveying the liturgical texts to our consciousness. The late Archimandrite Matthew (Mormyl') called this manner of presenting the text "high style." Let's briefly discuss the essence of *chitok* singing.

Chitok is a choral recitative used to sing lengthy liturgical texts (mainly stichera, troparia, hirmoi, and sometimes psalms). It is characterized by the singing of many words on one chord. Strictly speaking, the term *chitok* can be applied to any syllabic singing that involves minimal chanting of words: i.e., when maximum one or two sounds fall on one syllable. The name *chitok* began to be used relatively recently, to describe the special nature of the performance of choral recitative, distinguished by impeccable rhythmic, tempo, and dynamic evenness. The formation of this character of singing was gradual, and we can only talk about it in a hypothetical way—as about everything that is formed in the deep recesses of oral tradition. But according to some surviving records, as well as the testimonies of contemporaries, it can be said that the choir master of the Synodal Choir V. S. Orlov practiced this style of singing "psalmic" hymns, and was imitated in this by his later followers V. S. Komarov and N. V. Matveev. However, it was embodied most powerfully in the work of Archimandrite Matthew and the Lavra choir led by him. The value of this character of singing lies in the more convenient achievement of expressiveness and clarity of the sung text.

Since in worship the word and its meaning are primary, and the crucial issue is that the meaning of words must intelligibly reach the consciousness of the worshipers, in *chitok* style singing hymns must be performed with the utmost clear articulation. One must use the most powerful supported breathing for maximum legato. At the same time, there is no time signature and division into measures. The musical phrase is completely dependent on the length of the textual phrases. The sung words should sound with the same evenness and the following comparison is appropriate here: In each musical phrase, the words should be strung like pearls on a string. Here, maximum coordination is needed so that the singers feel, as it were, the pulse of the phrase as one person, without slowing everyone down and without pulling ahead. In fact, the choir should become, as it were, one person—a reader, a canonarch, smoothly reading the text. The main distinguishing feature of *chitok* is its evenness, for the optimal transmission of the word.

With the inept performance of *chitok*, one can completely deprive the singing of expressiveness, and even fall into some decadence and direct pathology. The sad distortion of *chitok* is observed when its performers sing staccato (or semi-staccato), which gives the sound the impression of completely inappropriate automatism and unnecessary yelling. In practice, the singing of *chitok* is characterized by the following:

1. There is no musical meter at all. It is absent.

2. The length of the phrase depends on the text, not the number of notes.

3. The "pulse" of this chant is even. Speeding up or slowing down is discouraged.

4. All the singers feel this pulse all the time.

5. The singing should not devolve into automatism. We are humans, not robots.

In conclusion, we want to remind you that we touched on this issue not as something mandatory, but as something recommended, for those who are up to this task, which is not everyone. And also so that you would be aware of the fact that such a phenomenon exists.

§ 8
The Choice of Liturgical Repertoire

When choosing works for singing at the service, the choir director should be guided not by his whim, but by common sense. Here we offer some practical considerations on this issue.

1. **Do not take pieces that are too complex.** It is not uncommon for some choir directors, especially beginners, to choose pieces that are beyond the capacity of the choir. Everyone wants to sing "something special." This leads to sad consequences. As a result, the worshipers listen not to well-performed spiritual music, but to the rehearsal of the choir, a sound that is not at all pretty, but out of tune out of rhythm, and without the proper artistic finish. Such singing is a mockery of those who pray, especially those who are not fortunate enough to have an ear for music and aesthetic sensitivity. But in general, this is ugly and irresponsible in relation to the church in general, and to one's own parish in particular. For example, we know a parish in which the choir director is very fond of a festive concert by Bortnyansky and really wants to sing it. But the voices are not there, and the choir is not capable of performing this piece correctly. For a number of years, year to year, during the festive period, this unfortunate concert is tormented and tormented, and with it the parishioners are tormented as well, and no one can finish the whole thing off in any way (finish off the concert,

that is, not the parishioners), because the choir director constantly tries to bring it back to life, but can neither learn how to perform it well, nor how to part with him. To solve this seemingly unsolvable task, we can offer the only available way out: set a specific goal with your choir – to learn this concert, and increase the number of rehearsals (which, by the way, are held very "symbolically" in the named parish after Sunday Liturgy, not even every week, but perhaps once every few months). With such a formulation of the matter, it is not surprising that this poor Bortnyansky concert has been "tortured" for so long, but cannot once and for all "give up the ghost." The point here is that success here is impossible without hard work. Here you must remember the saying that "art requires sacrifice." If there is hard work, and the desired result is achieved, the choristers (and the choir director, if he is not an absolute dummy – sometimes this happens, too) will have a sense of satisfaction and pride in the work done, which will greatly lift the spirit in the choir and will contribute to the development of further "musical Everests."

2. **On sentimentality and spirituality in church music.** This topic is directly related to the choice of repertoire. The topic is quite abstract, as a result of which people with little experience in church life often confuse one concept with another. In chapter 9 we will touch upon the influence music and its individual elements have on a person, in creating this or that mood. Indeed, the emotional attachment to something "pretty" or heartrending under the influence of some melody or harmonic arrangement, and creating a desired mood in oneself, testifies to the **sentimentality** of a work. At the same time, often the music does not correspond to the performed text. And this influx of emotions is often falsely perceived by a person almost as some kind of internal spiritual "illumination." On the other hand, **"spirituality"** implies an inner stability associated with the concepts of "sobriety" and "dispassion" so valued in the spiritual life. And various emotional/sentimental "insights" are interpreted in the spiritual life as spiritual self-delusion, disastrous for the soul.

The concepts of spirituality are most consonant with the spirit of our system of eight tones, which is why it is the main core of our church singing. Sentimentality, on the other hand, has firmly ingrained itself into the body of our church singing since the eighteenth century under the influence of the foreign influence of the Petrine era, and has introduced a major spiritual dissonance into the life of the Russian Church, with melodies that are completely alien to it and not at all appropriate for worship, often taken from secular music. We should emphasize that not all aspects of Western European influence on our church music life have been negative. When it comes to sentimentality/spirituality, the negative consequences are clear, but at the same time the Western influence contributed to the development of a rich legacy of choral performance practice, which became specifically Russian and has yet to be rivaled anywhere in the world, a fact widely acknowledged. Still, our co-religionists from other local churches have been more fortunate, in that they have managed to escape these internal contradictions. As for composed works, they are directly prohibited by church councils (the Council in Trullo and the 7th Ecumenical Council), but under the influence of the general secularization of our church life, no one takes this into account, and everyone very conveniently "forgets" about it. We have been infected by cultured Europe with a "spiritually indecent" disease of sentimentality, as a result of which many are ready to accept any banal rococo as some kind of "spiritual illumination." As an example of this, we cite Vedel's "Open unto me the gates of repentance." Or compare the text of the Pentecost stichera "Glorious things have been said today" in the interpretation of Dekhtyarev with the same text set to chant by the Trinity-Sergius Lavra in the arrangement of Hieromonk Nathanael. The choir director must keep such considerations in mind.

3. **Will the chosen piece encourage or hinder prayer?** There is a popular belief that there can be no dispute about tastes. The same applies to the sphere of church art, both visual and singing. By what criteria should we be guided in this matter? At one time, the ever-memorable Metropolitan Philaret (Voznesensky; †1985), in a conversation about icon-painting styles, was asked whether he prefers the ancient style of iconography or the more recent style. He answered that any icon is good for him, if only he can pray well before it. The same criterion applies to church singing, when considering free

compositions for performance in the church. It is necessary to clearly define whether a given work contributes to the prayerful mood of the parishioners or will be an obstacle to it. Also, when evaluating a particular free composition, the question always inevitably arises of how "churched" this work is, i.e., the degree to which it corresponds to the spirit of Orthodox worship and the traditional liturgical and aesthetic norms established in our church life, which determine the "churchness" or the appropriateness of performing this or that hymn in church. In order to prevent abuses in choral performance, the Typicon gives a warning in its 28th chapter "On unruly shouts," which repeats the 75th canon of the Sixth Ecumenical Council about this topic (see appendix 8).

It should be reiterated that the basis of Orthodox liturgical singing, which determines its inner spirit and general orientation, is the system of eight tones, presented in our monophonic Obikhods in its various versions, Znamenny (great and small), Greek, Kievan, Bulgarian chants. Thus, the measure for comparison—"a test for churchness"—is our Obikhod. If a free composition is stylistically sharply dissonant with the general sound ambiance of the church, then it should be treated with caution.

In judgments about the various styles of Russian church music, one should not go to extremes. For example, by the beginning of the twentieth century in Russia there was a return to the Russian folk musical roots in the works of the composers of the Moscow School or the so-called "New Direction," in opposition to the previously dominant influence of the Italian and German schools of composition. In church circles, contemptuous comments about "Italianism" in church singing were often heard at this time. But such comments were not always warranted. For example, once, at a rehearsal in the presence of Archimandrite Matthew (Mormyl), one of his leading singers disparaged Bortnyansky's work. "To this, Father Matthew responded quietly, but weightily: 'What do you know? Bortnyansky was possibly the most faithful Christian man of his time'."[3] Of course, the work of Bortnyansky, who studied music in Italy, naturally bore the imprint of Western influence, but the same Bortnyansky

---

[3] A. Betina, *I Sing to My God as Long as I Have My Being*, Sergiev Posad, 2019

wrote the hirmoi of the Great Canon "My helper and defender," without which our Lenten services are inconceivable, as well as many other things: "Beneath your compassion," "Come let us bless Joseph," "The Royal Cherubic Hymn No. 7," and others. It was no longer Italy that sounded here, but that rich musical atmosphere of Malorossiya, where the composer came from.

Below (in chapter 10) we will touch on the issue of diversity in worship, and on ways to overcome the boring monotony that parishioners sometimes complain about. Much in this case also depends on the selection of the repertoire by the choir director for performance in the church. The concept of diversity should not be confused with a heterogeneity of styles, i.e., when the Divine Liturgy is not a harmonious, unified whole, but rather resembles a colorful patchwork quilt.

Orthodox worship, both spiritually and artistically, is one, unified whole, having its own form and character. The parishioners, upon leaving the temple after the service, carry away with themselves a single, integral state of mind, inspired in part by the musical elements they heard, the melody, harmony, and rhythm. Here it is very important to perform the service in a uniform style. Otherwise, the worshiper will leave the temple not with peace of mind, but rather in a state of inner turmoil.

4. **The stylistic organization of the divine services.** An important factor in this case is the ratio of tonalities that sound in the temple. If possible, abrupt transitions from one key to another should be avoided, and in case of a change, one should stick to close, related modes: dominant, subdominant, or related minor. These serve as a kind of unifying element for everything that is performed in the temple. When planning a service, it can be musically divided into several integrally perceived sound "blocks." A possible variant of such a division is proposed:

For the Divine Liturgy:

1st block – The Great Litany, Antiphons, and Beatitudes can be adjusted to the tone in which the troparia will be sung, so that they are tonally united. Here it is important to keep to one style—either the work of similar composers or monastic settings—in such a way that there is no variegation of sound.

2nd block – Independent: Troparia, prokeimena, and Alleluia – here were at the mercy of the Obikhod melodies.

3rd block – The Cherubic Hymn, the Creed, the Mercy of Peace, It is truly meet, Our Father. In creating this sound block, follow the same principles as in the first block.

A note about the singing of the Lord's Prayer: The words of this prayer are so holy and deep that free compositions to this text are seen by us as simply blasphemous and indecent, and therefore sinful. We see the Rimsky-Korsakov version as the only exception to the more widespread option of singing it Obikhod style, precisely because of its simplicity and lack of sophisticated contortions. Another possible option for the Lord's Prayer is the Znamenny Chant version, for the same reason. By the way, in the Eastern churches this text is not sung, but read.

4th block – The end of the liturgy. According to the Typicon, the so-called communion verse is sung. Sometimes there are two of them, depending on the day being celebrated. Although music for these verses exists in the notated Obikhod, and they are in fact available in four-part harmonizations, unfortunately, they are usually performed in recitative on one note. This, to some extent, impoverishes worship. Furthermore, the duration of communion of the clergy in the altar depends on the number of serving clergy. If one priest serves, then he may have time to receive communion during the singing of the communion verse, especially if there are two verses. If the liturgy is episcopal or if several priests concelebrate, then communion in the altar usually takes more time. After the communion verse has been sung, to avoid a long pause during which parishioners often engage in inappropriate conversations, various chants of your choice may be sung. And even better, to help parishioners avoid empty conversations, one may occupy them with congregational singing; for this, well-known chants like "Beneath your compassion," "We have no other help than you," "My most-gracious Queen," or Psalms 50 or 90—the first in the arrangement of Archimandrite Matthew, the second according to the "Novo-Diveevo version" (acording to some sources, this is the Carpathian Tone 5)—are very suitable. Both psalms 50 and 90 are characterized by two alternating simple musical phrases, according to the question-answer scheme, and are easily learned by the singing congregation. To make this happen smoothly, the choir sings the first few words, which are then picked up by the congregation.

Also, at this point in the service one may sing various stichera taken from the All-Night Vigil for the day, or festive hirmoi (Pascha, Christmas, etc.). If there is a noticeable delay in communion at the altar, which happens, then you can read prayers for Holy Communion. The above-mentioned liturgical hymns should be stylistically and harmonically chosen according to the principles outlined above.

A kind of core that unites the blocks and runs through the entire liturgy is the litanies: the Great, the Augmented, and the two Supplicatory. They should be sustained in a uniform style—either monastic or compositional, this does not matter—but it is important that at the same time the internal integrity of the sound and emotional state be preserved.

A Note about Congregational Singing

It is a useful and pious custom have the congregation sing certain things together. At the Liturgy, this most often refers to: the Creed, the Lord's Prayer, and "Receive the Body of Christ." At one time, back in the 1960s, at Holy Trinity Monastery in Jordanville, it became customary for all of the people to sing together beginning with "The Father and the Son and the Holy Spirit" and continuing up to and including the communion verse. Both choirs, right and left, went out to the middle of the church, formed a semicircle and sang together. The people, standing right there and filling the church, sang along with the choir. The prayerful upsurge was felt by everyone. After the communion verse, the whole church often sang "Beneath your compassion," "Before your holy icon," or something else festive and well-known. At this time, communion of the clergy took place. By the time the laity received communion, the singers returned to the choir. So the block of congregational singing occupied a significant part of the Liturgy (up to 30 or 40 minutes). Such singing is practiced from time to time in Jordanville at various church celebrations to this day.

The All-Night Vigil can be built according to the same principles. Congregational singing is possible for the Megalynaria, "Having beheld the resurrection of Christ," and at the artoclasia, for the second repetition of the troparion of the feast when it is sung three times. To give the right "direction" to congregational singing, the choir can sing a few initial phrases (e.g., "I believe" or "Our Father"), and the people can pick up from there.

§ 9
The Choice of Repertoire:
The Influence of Music on a Person

The issue of choosing the liturgical repertoire is closely related to the issue of the influence on the listener of both music as a whole and of its individual facets: rhythm, melody, harmony, as well as its secondary elements, such as dynamics and tempo. Even in ancient times, philosophers such as Socrates, Plato, and Aristotle recognized the enormous influence of music on the human soul and introduced music into the subjects they felt necessary for the optimal education of a well-rounded person of that era. The early fathers of Christianity, both in the East and in the West, devoted a lot of time to this topic as well. They carefully classified the existing musical modes (which turned into the eight-tone system) and determined their suitability for church use. Clement of Alexandria indicated which modes were acceptable for use in worship, and which ones should be avoided, mainly those associated with Bacchic rites. Moreover, the early Fathers determined in detail which emotions were inherent in each mode. Tertullian also dealt with these issues, as well as the Hieromartyr Ignatius the God-bearer, who, incidentally, was the first to introduce the practice of antiphonal singing in the Church. In our time, these questions are also pertinent. For example, such a subtle observer as His Beatitude Metropolitan Anastassy commented on the relationship between music and prayer: "Prayer is the highest expression of the human spirit on earth, often striving to embody itself in harmonious musical sounds, which not only serve as beautiful clothes for it but are also wings that lift it up to heaven, where the jubilant singing never ceases—this constant language of the angels."[4] Even medical practice has addressed this topic. In my memory, there lived and worked in Munich Professor Ivan Shumilin, who dealt with the question of treating illnesses with music; he even came to America with lectures and, I remember, read them in our parish in Nyack.

The main elements of music are very diverse. Melodies can be cheerful (even playful), neutral, sad, tearful, sentimental, sugary-sweet. In a word, there is a whole range of possible created moods. Harmony is mostly either dissonant or consonant. The difference depends on the softness or abruptness of the introduced dissonances and how they are resolved. This also affects the internal sensations one experiences when listening to music. The most basic element—rhythm—creates either inner peace, evenness of sound, or anxiety and inner discomfort by shifting natural accents. Ultimately, the choir director must consider these factors, as relating to the state of mind in which the worshiper will leave the church. And for this he or she is responsible before God. Related to this is the topic of the culture of vocal sound; one cannot sing beautiful chants with an ugly sound. The choir director is also obliged to understand this side of the matter. Let us compare church singing with iconography. Let us imagine the well-known icon of the Holy Trinity by St. Andrei Rublev, painted with wondrous purity of colors. And here we have two copies in front of us: one is written immaculately so that it is impossible to distinguish from the original, and the second, preserving the composition and general contours, is painted by some incompetent painter using dirty, blurry colors and is an ugly parody of the original. The same applies to the field of church singing. No matter how beautiful the composition may be, if it is performed with out-of-tune, dissonant voices, it will result in the same ugliness. One must under no circumstances spoil beautiful music with bad voices. Here you need to accurately intone and control the emotional mood, which will be transmitted to the listeners.

---

[4] Metropolitan Anastassy, *Conversations with Your Own Heart*, Jordanville, 1998, p. 106.

§ 10
On Diversity in the Services

More than 1500 years ago, St. John Chrysostom, commenting about liturgical music, expressed the following thoughts, which are still fully applicable today.

> *What is singing for? Listen. When God saw that most men were slothful, that they came unwillingly to spiritual readings, and that they found the effort involved to be distasteful, wishing to make the labor more grateful and to allay its tedium he blended melody with prophecy in order that, delighted by the modulation of the chant, all might raise sacred hymns to him with great eagerness. For nothing so uplifts the mind, giving it wings and freeing it from the earth, releasing it from the prison of the body, affecting it with love of wisdom, and causing it to scorn all things pertaining to this life, as modulated melody and the divine chant composed of number (Exposition of Psalm 41).*

So wrote this hierarch 16 centuries ago. The weakness of human nature has not changed since those days, and, even if it has changed, then probably for the worst, and we have become even more slothful when it comes to divine services. This is in fact the source of the question of adding elements to our services that "delight by the modulation of the chant." Indeed, one often hears complaints even from regular church goers that the services are monotonous and drab. And what to say of those who have recently come to the church and are not yet ready for the "solid food" of spiritual ascetic struggle?

We must admit that, unfortunately, the repertoire of sacred music selection in many churches is very monotonous and quite predictable. In one central and otherwise quite successful parish, for example, the same setting of the proemial Psalm by Allemanov was sung for several decades in a row at the All-night Vigil, both for Sundays and feasts. And yet there are dozens or more compositions and arrangements of this Psalm that could and should be alternated at the services. At the same parish at the Divine Liturgy, before the reading of the Gospel Lesson, the same Alleluia in the "Moscow melody" is sung every single time, as if the Alleluia melodies set in the eight tones do not exist at all. The music framing the reading of the Gospel every week is that of Mokriants, because for many years the choir conductor was an émigré from Belgrade and the singers simply didn't know there was any other option. And yet, the Alleluia has the function of a prokimenon before the Gospel, and according to the Typicon should be sung in the indicated tone. Incidentally, the same variety of tones is indicated during the Sunday All-night Vigils, where "Holy is the Lord Our God" should also be sung to the tone of the week. And if a parish choir, in addition to ignoring the variety just described, relies on the *Obikhod* of Bakhmetev, with its tasteless "court melody," where many elements of hymnography (for example, the prokimena), are sung on one chord with the final cadence I-IV-V-I, while singing all Litanies according to the schema "C-A-F," the picture of the complete decline of liturgical performance practice becomes clear.

The reason for this decline is rooted in the fact that many choir directors and precentors are unfamiliar with the melodic richness of our monophonic *Obikhods* (described in chapter 2). Precisely these books should serve as the source for melodies in the cases described above. If the choir director has a musical education and is able to write out harmonizations and arrangements of the melodies printed in these monophonic *Obikhods*, so much the better. Otherwise, he or she can turn to a more experienced colleague in the nearest parish for help, or, if this is not possible, look for the necessary material in one of many compendia published now in Russia and widely available in bookstores and on the internet.

In addition to widening the repertoire, let us now discuss a series of measures that can naturally add appropriate liveliness to the Divine services. This should, of course, be done in consultation with the rector and only with his blessing.

We propose:

At the All-night Vigil:

1. At the reading of the canon, alternate readers for the Troparia and refrains of canons. That is, one reader reads the refrains, and the second reader reads the Troparia.

2. In the same fashion, one can alternate the readers of stichera and their verses. This is in those cases, where the singing of stichera is problematic due to the lack of competent singers. It is better to read the stichera well, than to sing them sloppily with dubious diction and intonation. However, in those cases, where there are competent singers capable of performing the stichera well, even in a quartet, it is of course preferrable to sing them, which greatly livens the service and gives those attending a certain "pick me up."

3. Where it is possible and practical, it is good to introduce the practice of singing certain stichera, at least those at "Glory" and "Both now," with a Canonarch. The congregation may also join this type of singing.

4. Singing with a Canonarch the first sticheron of the evening Litē during the procession of the clergy out of the Altar into the Narthex on the eves of great feasts highlights the festivity of the moment and brings out the meaning of the feast for the congregation.

5. It is possible to introduce congregational singing at some points in the All-night Vigil, for example, the Troparion at the Blessing of the Loaves, alternating with the clergy; the Megalynaria; and the hymn "Having beheld the resurrection of Christ" at the Saturday night vigils.

6. At the Saturday night vigils, we suggest singing the Hymns of Ascents either in the tone of the week or to a quality composition of the appropriate ecclesiastical style. Here the work of Metropolitan Jonathan (Yeletskikh) may be suggested; these compositions are not complicated and sound quite prayerful.

7. At the Sunday vigil, singing the Primary Theotokion (Dogmaticon) in Znamenny chant in unison (if the choir has the necessary number and quality of male voices) is unusual and augments the festivity of the moment. But this should only be attempted if the choir can perform this hymn well.

8. It would be good to introduce the practice of singing the prosomoea (*podobni*) to their automela melodies, which give the hymnography a very specific, festive character. One should not be afraid of the automela; they are not at all difficult, and the music for them may be found in the *Precentor's Companion*, as well as the square-notes

Octoechos. We highly recommend turning your attention to this wealth of melodic repertoire.

9. The sticheron "All-blessed art thou, O Theotokos Virgin" before the Great Doxology at the Saturday night vigil is usually sung in tone 2, since this text is printed in the Octoechos as a Sessional Hymn in that tone. Nonetheless, the sticheron is sung every week. In some parishes (for example, the "Joy of All Who Sorrow" cathedral in San Francisco), the practice is to sing the sticheron in the tone of the week. This practice makes the service noticeably livelier, and there is nothing wrong with it.

10. In the Russian Orthodox Church there is a tradition of singing the Kontakion for the Theotokos "To Thee, the Champion Leader" at the end of the First Hour. This tradition emerged in Muscovite Rus after the miraculous delivery of the city of Moscow from the Tatar hordes through the intercession of the Theotokos. Other local Orthodox Churches do not have this tradition, and the text is not printed in our Horologion. In many cathedrals, including the "Joy of All who Sorrow" Cathedral in San Francisco, as well as in Russia, the text of "To Thee, the Champion Leader" is replaced by the Kontakion for the feast during feasts and their afterfeasts up until the Apodosis. In all other cases "To the Thee Champion Leader" is sung.

At the Divine Liturgy:

1. At the Liturgy, by comparison with the All-night Vigil, singing is interrupted by reading less frequently and the reading is different in character—Sacred Scripture and litanies; consequently, the Liturgy may be understood is a musical monolith with a specific tonal coloration and form. So, when selecting the repertoire for the Liturgy, it is very important to consider the character of each composition and to see how well they agree one with another in key, tempo, overall sound, and other parameters. The widespread formula for repertoire — Kastalsky, Bortnyansky, L'vov, Chesnokov — is not always successful when choosing music for any more or less festive Liturgy (particularly a hierarchical service). The congregation should not only receive the fruits of the grace of the Holy Spirit at the Liturgy, but also

be edified by a holistic musical sound, which will be firmly imprinted in the consciousness and continue to accompany the individual congregants during the course of the day (see ch. 7, on the choice of liturgical repertoire).

2. The reading or singing (the latter is preferred) of the Troparia at the Beatitudes serves to bring out the meaning of the feast.

3. Congregational singing at Liturgy raises the over level of prayerfulness for the People of God present in the Church. If deacons with good voices are available, they are usually given the task of guiding the congregation. Commonly, the Creed and the Lord's Prayer are sung with the congregation.

4. The Prokimena and Alleluia should be sung in their appropriate tone. Even within one tone, there is a fairly wide set of possible melodies: Znamenny, Kievan, Greek, Kiev Caves, and others.

5. Those who seek to follow as closely as possible the rubrics indicated by the Typicon can succeed in this by singing the coenonicon (communion verse) to the melodies placed in the monophonic Obikhod. There is likewise a large selection of these melodies. For example, the Sunday coenonicon "Praise the Lord from the heavens" is given in four versions: a. Znamenny chant; b. "Another" melody; c. Kievan chant; d. "Yet Another" melody. The coenonica for feasts and weekdays are also notated in different melodies. In this way, one can avoid the situation where, after singing the coenonicon on one chord with the usual cadence – I-IV-V-I – one is forced to ask the choir members, "What should we sing now, 'O fervrent intercession' by Chesnokov or 'Unto the Theotokos let us flee' by Arkhangelsky?"

§ 11
Concerning Abbreviations in Liturgical Practice

The question of liturgical abbreviations is a purely pastoral one, and its resolution lies squarely with the rector of the parish. Thus, this question is not one for the choir director, who must in this case only follow the rector's directions. The rector, after all, bears the responsibility before God for the spiritual formation of a larger spiritual family, the parish. And in this question, he must be guided by considerations for the greater good, which may be distilled in only one concern: "do no harm" to the spiritual state of the parishioners. Considerations of strictness or leniency need to be balanced, depending on the circumstances. On the one hand, an approach that is too lenient may completely degrade the parishioners; on the other, exceeding strictness can drive them away altogether, and then you might as well simply close the parish. Experienced spiritual elders remind us, that all people make mistakes. And the priest in this case is not an exception – he will also make mistakes. At the same time, it is in the general spirit of Christianity to make mistakes in the direction of leniency rather than strictness (according to Archbishop Andrei [Rymarenko], d. 1978). The judicious use of the "weapon of goodwill" is much more effective than a clumsily conducted politics of the "carrot and stick," multiplied (as it often is) by the "syndrome of the rector's infallibility." The priest must account for this in all aspects of parish life, including the liturgical.

Russian believers tend to be conservative, and this conservatism is often particularly obvious on the kliros. One experienced pastor once commented as follows: "There's a bit of the Old Believer in all of us." And we should not forget this tendency. There is an opinion that for the Old Believer, the most important book in Christianity is not the Gospel but the Typicon. A similar tendency may be seen among some of our cliros enthusiasts, who suffer from "mindless zealotry." Let us avoid this if we at all can.

The question of the abbreviation of services, furthermore, is only one facet of a broader painful phenomenon in church life, characterized by the ever-memorable Archbishop Vitaly (Maksimenko) as "Eastern-rite Protestantism"—namely, a widespread secularization of church life, which has, like a wide wave, swept the Orthodox world in the United States. Outwardly, this process is expressed in the violation of church discipline, both spiritual and liturgical: the weakening or even abolition of fasting; the change to the Gregorian calendar; the distortion of the Typicon; the abbreviation of worship; the installing of benches and even organs after the western manner in churches; the abolition of the liturgical veil, and with it, sometimes, the Holy Doors; and the suppression of traditional attire for clergy. Thus we see a certain "McDonaldization" of Orthodoxy.

The question of the abbreviation of services in parishes of the Russian Orthodox Church Outside of Russia is rather complicated. There is no unanimity in this sense among the hierarchy or the clergy, or among the parishioners. Some believers consider any such reductions to be sinful, correctly remarking that it is an arbitrary mutilation of worship, in violation of its internal structure, that indulges the inner spiritual laxity and laziness of clergy and singers. Many parishioners and worshipers believe that such reductions are an unacceptable undermining of ecclesiastical discipline, and their position can be formulated like this: "We are in the ROCOR, and this is not acceptable!" In other words, "If you want a brief service—go to the modernists!"

Nonetheless, the problem does exist. It manifests itself most obviously in the ever-decreasing attendance at services in our churches, especially at the All-Night Vigil. There is a direct connection between the length of these services and the number of people who attend them. The general conclusion is evident: the longer the service, the fewer people remain to the end or even to the mid-point. As the well-known American expression goes, people "vote with their feet." In those parishes where the Vigil lasts over three hours, the church is, in most cases, sparsely attended. On the other hand, if Vigil lasts 2 to 2½ hours, the attendance is usually quite a bit better.

So, on the one hand we have the fundamental requirement, dictated by our ecclesiastical conscience, of keeping to the prescribed order and, on the other hand, there are practical considerations of a pastoral nature about how to not lose worshipers during the service. The resolution of this pastoral dilemma is the immediate responsibility of our hierarchy. It should be noted that, however, the hierarchy is not very inclined to pursue this matter, at least not at the present moment. In the past, the issue was raised at the Council of Bishops in 1950, but neither then, nor in subsequent years, has a clear solution been proposed.

Still, the conciliar decision in 1950 does deserve mention. It is outlined in a fairly detailed manner in a separate brochure printed by Holy Trinity Monastery in 1951. This brochure should be reprinted because of the beautiful and deep views expressed in it, which are still relevant in our day. The discussion at the Council came down basically to two main points of view.

1. Bishop Gregory (Borishkevich) of Montreal (d. 1956) pointed out that the topic of abbreviating services was on the agenda at the Moscow Council of 1917–18. That Council, recognizing the need for strict adherence to the Typicon in the monasteries and cathedrals, admitted to the possibility of abbreviating the services in parish churches, since an overly strict stringency in this matter may lead to adverse results. Therefore, Bishop Gregory concluded that "there is a need to have two 'normal' Typica: a monastery Typicon for monasteries and cathedrals and a parish Typicon for other parishes of the Diaspora; this latter would take into account the state of affairs among our laity, who are unable to devote as much time and attention to the temple."[5]

2. There followed a lively exchange of views, which came down to the conclusions that (a) any allowable cuts should be done with an understanding of the structure of the services; and that (b) "any authorization by the Council of a lighter Typicon as a new norm would not be appropriate, because in the absence of proper zeal, such a lighter Typicon would only lead to even further abbreviations in the services."

Summing up the views expressed, Metropolitan Anastassy (a member of the Moscow Council of 1917–18) said that the Moscow Council deliberately abandoned the idea of creating a shortened parish Typicon, fearing thereby to provide encouragement for further abuse and negligence. The resolution of the Council of Bishops on this subject is as follows:

Resolution of the Liturgical Commission of the Council of Bishops in 1950

"*Taking into account the fact that the church services are the very*

---

[5] "Kak Sobliudat' Tserkovny Ustav? Vopros ob yedinoobrazii tserkovnogo bogosluzheniya na Arkhiereiskom Sobore Russkoi Pravoslavnoi Tserkvi Zagranitsei," Jordanville, 1951.

breath of Church life and have been handed down to the Church by the divinely inspired Church Fathers for the edification, strengthening and sanctification of the children of the Church, and that their violation inevitably leads to a decline of spiritual life, the Council calls the clergy, singers and worshipers to more zealously respect the ecclesiastical Typicon, performing the services as completely as possible, with reverence and proper decorum. Where circumstances dictate a need to make abbreviations, these should be made with great care, not breaking the general structure of the service; this is to be overseen on the local level by diocesan bishops."[6]

Commission Chairman – Archbishop John of Shanghai

Thus, we see that this question has not yet been resolved to complete satisfaction, and our choir directors and singers have to somehow deal with it on the local level. Coming from personal experience, we can offer as a partial solution to this problem the order for serving the All-Night Vigil at the Holy Virgin Protection Church in Nyack, NY, where, for many years, the well-known Archpriest Seraphim Slobodskoy (d. 1971) was the Rector, and where the Saturday night service lasted 2½ hours. It was performed in an unhurried and diligent manner, without losing its general structure described in the Typicon.

The typical **All-night Vigil for Sunday or a feast** was served in the following manner:

1. **All of the fixed prayers** (including the Six Psalms) were done in full.

2. Abbreviations were allowed at the following points:

a) **The Cathismata** were abbreviated in accordance with the well-known scheme blessed by St. John of Shanghai, according to which all 23 Psalms of the first three cathismata are read during the course of the eight-week cycle of the Octoechos. (These were read only at Matins). Each Psalm counted as a "Glory."

---

[6] Ibid., p. 1.

Schema for abbreviating Sunday Cathismata, blessed by St. John

Sunday Tone	Psalms
1	1, 5, 9
2	2, 6, 10
3	3, 7, 11
4	4, 8, 12
5	13, 17(1–30), 17(31–46)
6	14, 18, 21
7	15, 19, 22
8	16, 20, 23

b) **Psalm 50** after the Polyeleos and Gospel Lesson was omitted, except for those instances when it is specifically indicated in the rubrics (for example, on the eves of Palm Sunday and Pentecost)

c) **The First Hour** began with the third psalm, "Of mercy and judgment."

d) **The hirmoi of the catabasia** were sung only at Odes 3, 6, 8, and 9 of the Canon. However, at the Vigil for the major feasts, the catabasiae were sung in full.

e) **Stichera** were sung in full, except in those cases were repetitions were indicated.

3. Stichera were sung in the following manner: the first sticheron and the sticheron at "both now and ever" were always sung by the choir. The other stichera were read clearly by readers, without rushing, so that the congregation would be able to hear and understand every word. To avoid monotony, a second reader would read the verses appointed between the stichera. This concerned the stichera at "Lord, I have cried," the Aposticha, the Litē, and the Praises.

4. At the Canon, all of the Troparia were read in full, again with the exception of cases where the rubrics indicate that a Troparion should be repeated. Again, to avoid monotony, one reader read the Troparia of the Canon while a second reader read the appointed verses.

At the **Divine Liturgy** there were no abbreviations, except the usual abbreviation of Psalm 102, which had come into practice as far back as the Synodal Notated Books of the pre-Revolutionary period. The Troparia at the Beatitudes were always read. Psalm 33 was omitted entirely.

In the above-mentioned scenario, no one complained about the length of the services. The length of the Vigil was acceptable without unacceptable abbreviations. In fact, often guests from other parishes commented on the strict adherence to the Typicon and even "monastic tendencies" of the services in Nyack.

We should also highlight the importance of reading the Troparia at the Beatitudes at the Divine Liturgy. It is very illogical and unfortunate that on feast days, for which the Liturgy, in fact, is being served, the only mention of the feast is in the Troparion and Kontakion, and, maybe, in the Gospel lesson (if it is a feast of the Lord). The rest of the Liturgy has many beautiful hymns, which are not movable and have no relation to the celebrated event. The Troparia from the Canon for the feast, which are executed at the Beatitudes (they can be read, or even better—sung), adequately fill this gap and turn the attention of the congregation to the celebrated event.

As for the reading of Psalm 50 at Matins, the initial words of this psalm are still sung, and they contain the main idea of the entire psalm. As for the remaining verses of the psalm, in spite of their spiritual loftiness and importance, they (especially if executed by ordinary monotonous reading) slip past the attention of the faithful. So, probably for this reason, in many of our churches this Psalm is omitted. At the Holy Trinity Monastery in recent years, a good practice has been established: during the period of the Lenten Triodion this psalm is sung completely, in the arrangement of the late Archimandrite Matthew. This custom is very laudable and worthy of emulation not just in monasteries but in parishes, where the psalm can be sung during the Lenten season. In conjunction with "Upon the waters of Babylon" and "Open unto me the gates of repentance," the singing of Psalm 50 is of great spiritual and educational value for our faithful, who in the case of Lenten services are unlikely to complain about the length of the service.

In conclusion, it should be reiterated that the question of abbreviating services is above all a pastoral issue. The notorious expression of the Typicon "If the Rector so desires," unfortunately, has served as the basis for a wide range of arbitrary decisions on the part of priests, who are not always distinguished by zeal in the matter of services and, at the same time, often are poorly educated.

However, in those places where the pastor pays scrupulous attention to the spiritual education of his parishioners, the resolution of these issues should not cause unnecessary disagreement and gossip. Everything can be done properly when both the pastors and the flock follow the precept of the Apostle Paul to the Corinthians: "Let all things be done decently and in order"[7] (even the abbreviation of services).

§ 12
The Element of Time in the Services

The memorable Father Paul Florensky envisioned the divine services not just as an art, but as the synthesis of all art forms. And indeed, in services in the temple we see the combination of both expressive and performance art. Expressive art here includes frescoes, icons, and architecture; performance art includes choreography (the movements of the clergy), poetry, composition, vocal arts (both choral and individual). Even the smoke of the censors, according to Father Paul, is an integral part of this complex of impressions. Expressive art is experienced in space; it is static (at the end of the day, a poorly painted icon can be corrected); for its part, performance art here is related to the time dimension, which means there is even more responsibility placed on those performing to do so to perfection, since if anything is done badly, the general negative impression remains. More than that, singers have the responsibility to remember the biblical injunction: "Cursed be the one who does the Lord's work negligently" (Jer. 48:10). This warning should at a minimum cause us to reflect on our responsibility.

All of the above may be thought of as general observations on the topic in this chapter. How does this practically apply to the work of the church

---

[7] 1 Cor. 14:40.

choir conductor? Quite directly. One of the main conditions for the solemn celebration of worship is its smooth flow. For this, the choir director needs to have a sense of proportion, a certain church-liturgical instinct that will prompt him or her to make the right decisions in matters of dynamics and tempo when performing music with the choir.

Both hasty singing, and singing that is excessively protracted for the sake of its supposedly prayerful character, should be avoided. In no case should we allow pauses in singing, even of the shortest kind. The congregants are negatively affected when a choir director gives the pitch repeatedly, and the choir enters uncertainly, sometimes several times, until the singing sounds more or less correctly. We must feel the liturgical moment and make the tempo of the singing accord with the actions of the clergy in the altar and the flow of the service in the church in general. Here we present the most typical cases of such "inconsistencies" encountered in our liturgical practice.

1. During the time of censing at the All-Night Vigil, that is, during: a) "Lord, I have cried"; b) the Polyeleos; and c) "More honorable," the choir director must constantly monitor where the censing clergyman is located. Has he finished going around the temple? If not, how much distance does he have to cover and how long will it take? At the same time, it is necessary to calculate how long the singing will take, in order for the ending of the censing to coincide with the ending of the singing.

2. At solemn festive vespers performed by a bishop in attendance (e.g., on Pentecost, Great Thursday and Saturday, forgiveness Sunday and other similar occasions) at the time of the Little Entrance, when the bishop is in the middle of the church on the cathedra and the clergy need to leave the altar and come to the middle of the church, a sticheron is sung at "Both now." It often happens that the distance from the altar to the middle of the church is significant, the sticheron is short, and the singers sing this sticheron too quickly. The sticheron is sung, the bishop is standing alone on the cathedra, and the clergy emerge from the altar in silence and with a guilty countenance. This happens because the choir director in general is not concerned about the coordination of the singing with the actions of the clergy.

3. The greeting of the bishop also requires much attention as far as the question of time is concerned. What matters here is the speed of the bishop's pace when walking, his personal habits when venerating the icons, as well as the pace of reading the Entrance Prayers by the Protodeacon. It often happens that the choir has sung "It is truly meet" completely, and the bishop has not yet had time to venerate all of the icons. Depending on the remaining fragment of time, you should: a) either repeat the "More honorable" or, b) if you can see that the procession is approaching its end, come in on the last phrase "True Theotokos, we magnify Thee."

4. When the Cherubic Hymn is performed, it is usually customary to perform the first three verses slowly, and this is quite appropriate for the liturgical moment, because at this time a number of important actions take place in the altar: prayers at the altar, censing, commemoration at the Table of Oblation. All this takes a lot of time, and sometimes you have to repeat individual phrases of the Cherubic Hymn several times to avoid silence (for example, when St. John of Shanghai served, it often happened that the Cherubic Hymn had to be repeated in full three times). However, after the great entrance, it is customary for some reason to perform the appointed "That we may receive the King of all" at an excessively fast pace, almost *allegro vivace*. We have here almost some kind of ridiculous tradition, and one that is not at all justified. Yes, solemnly, yes, loudly, but why such a lightning-fast pace? At this time in the altar, the sacred vessels prepared for the Bloodless Sacrifice are being set on the Altar Table. At the same time, a series of actions are carried out, which in their importance leave no room for haste. The swift singing of "That we may receive the King of all" in this case injects fussiness; the choir director should take this into account and, if possible, avoid it.

5. During the Divine Liturgy, especially during the Anaphora (Eucharistic Canon), one should not hurry with the choral responses to the exclamations of the priest. It must be remembered that during this singing the priest is reading the secret prayers. He needs to concentrate as much as possible, which is not at all promoted by a hurried reading of these prayers. Not all priests read at the same speed;

one is slower, one is faster. And not all of the settings of "Mercy of Peace" have the same duration. This applies particularly to the liturgies of St. Basil the Great, whose Eucharistic prayers are several orders of magnitude longer than those of St. John Chrysostom. It is necessary to consider the fact that the liturgy of St. Basil the Great is served only ten times a year and therefore its prayers are not only longer but less familiar to the serving priest than the prayers of the liturgy of Chrysostom. Therefore, to read them in a hurry, "just to keep up with the choir," is completely unacceptable. How many times did it happen in our practice that during the liturgy of St. Basil, the priest is still reading the prayers and the choir has already finished singing? There is a heavy silence in the temple that lasts up to a full minute, or even longer. In these cases, the pause feels like an eternity. From the choir, the director's impatient coughing can be heard, translated as "What are you doing there, father, that is taking so long?" And this at a moment when the priest should concentrate on praying and delving into the essence of the greatness of the sacrament being performed.

6. Another liturgical moment to which the director should pay attention: after the communion of the people, the Holy Gifts are brought into the altar and placed on the Holy Table. Then the prosphora particles on the diskos are immersed into the Holy Chalice. Again, this action should not be done hastily in order not to spill the particles onto the Antimension or, worse, spill the contents of the Chalice. During this same time Alleluia is sung, followed by "We have seen the true light." These chants should also not be sung too quickly.

In all the cases mentioned, common sense should dictate the proper course of action. Here we have indicated only the most widespread examples of what, in our opinion, requires correction in the current choir practice. Probably, many more such observations can be made.

§ 13
The Relationship between the Choir Director and the Rector

The quality of singing in any church largely depends on this relationship. Considering that the main purpose of church singing is to contribute to the prayer of the parishioners, it cannot be otherwise. It is good where the rector in his spiritual, cultural and intellectual qualities corresponds to his position. And where the choir director in his church and musical training—to his. However, life shows that this is not always the case. And this can cause a whole range of, to put it mildly, "rough spots."

Therefore, for some, this topic may also be titled as "what is the rector and how to deal with him." The topic is delicate, but relevant for many, so we will touch on it here.

After all, it must be borne in mind that in our cramped conditions as emigrants, priests often get their position just as accidentally as choir directors (when there is no one else, and there is a pious parishioner available). Most often, when looking for a candidate for a priestly position, the hierarchs look at his personal moral qualities, and whether he has any canonical obstacles to ordination. This is put at the forefront. Questions of spiritual upbringing and education recede into the background. And they ordain the candidate with the faith that the Divine Grace, "which healeth that which is infirm and completeth that which is wanting," will smooth out all the "uneven corners" in the ministry of this priest. And this faith in the power of God's grace is often not put to shame. Many worthy shepherds came to their ministry in this way. But to get a worthy candidate with a theological education in our time is simply a luxury. In any case, priests do not grow in our flower beds, either trained ones or ignoramuses. And how many in our time will agree to embark on this path of life, so thorny and difficult purely in everyday terms?

However, we have digressed somewhat from the topic. Bearing responsibility before God for all aspects of parish life, regardless of his qualifications, the priest is also responsible for singing. Or rather, for preventing the choir from performing hymns that run counter to the spirit of worship and interfere with prayer. There is another nuance here. Some of the most important hymns of the "Liturgy of the Faithful," such as the Cherubic hymn, the "Mercy of Peace," "It is truly meet," evoke a certain inner mood in the priest, like in any other person. Usually, there are no difficulties with hymns of Obikhod/monastic origin, although some composers sometimes manage to write in a "liturgical mood" that does not run counter to the spirit of the liturgical moment. It is more difficult when the choir sings some kind of free composition that goes against the prayerful mood of the serving priest, which distracts him from his direct work. And in these matters, his voice should be decisive, despite the choir director's efforts to perform some of his favorite hymns and thus ensure "the sweetness of the church." And then the offended choir director has no choice but to complain about the lack of culture and musical illiteracy of the priest. And here the matter is not in the musical, but in the spiritual sphere. Sometimes, the relationship deteriorates to such an extent that they do not communicate with each other at all. We will give an example known to us from real life, when the choir director-precentor, coming to the temple, did not go to the altar to greet the rector and take a blessing, but went to the choir loft, and at the appointed time defiantly cleared his throat, which in translation meant, "I am here, Father. It's time to start; give the blessing."

In order to avoid such ugly situations, the choir director and the rector should develop a mutual understanding, where the choir director should be guided by certain criteria set by the priest, and the priest, in turn, should be tactful about the musical efforts of the choir director and not step on his or her toes too much.

*

So far, we have dealt with questions of a general nature; now it is time for us to turn our attention to the purely technical side of the matter, without understanding of which our work will be flawed in many respects. Many of these aspects of our work connect to the subject of choral studies, but nevertheless there are some urgent topics (such as vocal technique) that are not included in the field of choral studies. We will touch on these issues in the second part of our textbook.

Part II:

Practical Considerations

§ 14
Some Information about the Vocal Apparatus

About the human voice in general

The human voice is a musical instrument. And although we usually do not perceive it as such, nevertheless it is so. Let's say more. Of all musical instruments, it is the most perfect since, while some violin or trumpet is the work of human hands, our voice is an instrument not made by hands, the creation of God Himself. The voice can convey the finest intonation nuances that are inaccessible to any instrument. This is exemplified in the nonlinear "hook" (neumatic) notation, which is vocal in nature and preserved in the Old Rite, in contrast to the five-line notation, designed for instrumental music and used everywhere in churches as well as in secular music. This instrument, the voice, was created on the principle of all existing musical instruments. All of them have three components:

1. A vibrating mass that sets the air in motion. In the human voice: **the vocal cords**. The singer has no direct control over them and should not think about them while singing.

2. The engine that sets the vocal cords in motion: the **breathing apparatus, diaphragm, abdomen, and intercostal muscle**. This is an essential ingredient in singing, so much so that there is a saying, "Learning to sing is learning to breathe." The fundamental work of the singer-vocalist is precisely in mastering this process. There is a vocal/instrumental comparison: "The singer plays with air (his breath) along the vocal cords, like a violinist with a bow on the strings." The comparison is quite accurate, and if the choir director is not a vocalist

himself and cannot teach his choir how to sing, then it is worth inviting an external vocal teacher and conducting a series of group lessons with the choir. Although breathing is central to singing, it is only indirectly related to the question of the culture of sound (see appendix 10). Therefore, let's move on to the topic of the formation of the sung sound, which occurs in the oral cavity.

3. The resonating cavity (*resonating chamber*), which carries the function of an amplifier. **In the human voice this is the oral cavity and larynx**. Also, the sinuses and chest are partially involved. All singing, in essences, takes place through the articulation of vowel sounds. Each vowel has its own specific form, which is formed depending on the position of the mouth, mainly the tongue and lips (see appendix 9).

It is not possible to give a detailed presentation of the whole physiological process of singing within the limits of this textbook. And this is not important, because you will not learn to sing merely by reading about singing, without practical exercises, just like you can't learn to drive a car just by reading a written driver's manual. Nevertheless, such instructions are necessary. Here we will touch on only one facet of this process, which is directly related to the vocal "beauty," and, consequently, to the beauty of church singing generally.

Here, for clarity, it is appropriate to compare the voice with a wind instrument, for example, with a brass horn (*trumpet*). This instrument is a copper pipe 12 feet long, for the convenience of playing, bent into the shape of a kind of pretzel, equipped with three valves that are pressed and released during playing. This changes the internal configuration (i.e., length) of the pipe, and, depending on this change, the pitch of the emitted sound also changes. The pipe itself remains motionless, and only the shape of the internal void through which air is supplied changes in it.

When forming vowel sounds, something similar happens with the singing apparatus. All five vowels (A, O, U, I, E) have a certain form of inner emptiness, depending on the position of the jaw, lips, and tongue. Through this void, air is sent from the lungs, setting the vocal cords in motion. Changing the shape of this void, as in a pipe, changes the sound—not the pitch, but the sounding vowel.

§ 15
On the Speaking and Singing Positions of the Vocal Apparatus

The singing position when giving a sound consists in the most naturally lowered larynx, with the soft palate raised in the position of a yawn. This position is called "pear-shaped" by English-speaking music critics (*Pear shaped sound*). This definition can be understood if we imagine that we have a pear in our mouth, the top of which protrudes from our mouth with a stalk. Its wide bottom pushes our larynx down with one side, and presses our soft palate up with the other side. Fortunately, this imagery, remaining in the imagination of critics, does not translate into reality. However, it does provide a fairly accurate description of the singing position, as this position maximizes our natural vocal resonance. The next time when your interlocutor when talking with you starts to yawn widely, and at the same time continue his speech without interruption, pay attention to how this will affect the sound of his voice. During a yawn, he will naturally sound one and a half to two times louder, due to an increase in the resonant space in his oral cavity *(resonance chamber)*. You can often recognize a singer by the sound of his conversation, because even in conversation their "instrument" is set up for singing. Many lecturers, educators, preachers who have to talk a lot in their line of work speak in a similar way. Often they turn to phoniatrists for help (*speech therapists*). Otherwise, they may be left without a voice. In the speaking position during vocalization, the soft palate is not raised and the larynx is not lowered. This robs the sound of the maximum possible resonance and lowers its vocal efficiency. In addition, when singing, this also negatively affects the timbre, significantly impoverishing its sound palette, and produces the so-called white sound (from the French *voix blanche*). This is how an open, flat, unpleasant, singing (or rather anti-singing) sound is characterized by choristers who "sing" in a conversational position.

§ 16
Timbre

The concept of timbre means individual coloring (*tone color*) of the singing sound, which is unique and unrepeatable for each person. There are timbres similar to one another, but two identical timbres do not exist, just as there are no identical fingerprints. Each voice, subjected to analysis through special equipment, will give out its own individual sound "imprint", by which it is possible to determine who is singing or speaking. A. I. Solzhenitsyn, in his First Circle, built the main plot of the work around this axis.

Timbre is the characteristic sound of a voice by which you can recognize a person without even seeing him, and how the color of hair or eyes is given to everyone by nature. Timbre can be beautiful or ugly, pleasant or nasty, annoying or soothing, bright or dull. The work of vocal teachers, in addition to the goal of setting the voice, often comes down to "putting makeup on" ugly timbres. Let's take an example. It is known from the memoirs of contemporaries that the famous Russian composer Mikhail Ivanovich Glinka by nature was the owner of a "lousy tenor." But he also loved to sing. And through hard work with teachers, he became an excellent performer of romances, which his friends gathered with pleasure to listen to.

§ 17
Some Tips for Rehearsing the Choir

In order for church singing to be magnificent, it is not at all necessary to have powerful bright voices in the choir. Experience shows that the opposite is often the case, since such voices tend to stand out from the general choral texture. The main thing to strive for is a coherent sound, what is called an "ensemble" in the musical environment, in which, in the presence of many singers, individual voices do not stand out. It should not be forgotten that the human voice is a musical instrument, moreover, the most perfect instrument, since it was created not by man, but by God. Furthermore, it can be said that the choir, consisting of these voices, is to an even greater extent a musical instrument, which an experienced director should "be able to play." The main work on the choral sound should take place in the rehearsals of the choir, which should not be neglected. At such rehearsals, the work on "choral instrument tuning," i.e. choral vocals, is no less important than learning new pieces.

About choir rehearsals – general provisions:

1. Rehearsals should be carried out as regularly as possible, and the

singers should be educated to realize the importance of their work and have a sense of responsibility before God and the parish for the quality of their work.
2. It is important to consider the place and time of rehearsals. Where singers for the most part live within easy reach of the church, rehearsals can be scheduled at any time convenient for everyone. In cases where many choristers live at a considerable distance from the church, it is more convenient to hold rehearsals at times close to the services, for example, after the Sunday Liturgy, either in the church or in the church hall.
3. Rehearsals should not be lengthy. The optimal duration of the rehearsal is 30 to 40 minutes, and in any case no more than an hour. (Especially when the amateur choir has just sung the Liturgy and is already tired).
4. The director must consider the state of the choir, the time of day, and which of the choristers have come to the rehearsal.
5. During rehearsals, you should focus on problematic places in the works you are learning. The director himself must know all the parts in order to be able to show with his voice how this or that place is sung. Also, he must thoroughly know and feel the whole work, and teach it to the singers. He should not use rehearsal time to learn the piece himself and torment the choir with endless repetitions.
6. Each rehearsal must be thought out in advance by the director so that there is no waste of time. It is also necessary to not just focus on the upcoming rehearsals but also to have a longer-term work plan, taking into account both the upcoming festal hymns and the expansion of the liturgical repertoire in general, useful for the musical development of the choir.

On the methods of working with the choir:

1. The rehearsal should begin with exercises that develop proper breathing as the basis of any vocalization.
2. This should be followed by singing vocalizes aimed at

strengthening the voice and expanding its range.
3. Also important are exercises that develop the musical ear and the ability to hear the surrounding singers, as well as to hear yourself in the ensemble.
4. With amateur singers who don't sight-read music very well, which is the majority of singers in our choirs, when learning an unfamiliar work, for its faster learning, it is recommended to separate its main elements, **text, rhythm, and melody**. These elements should be first learned separately, and then combined. For example:

a. First, just read the **text** together with the whole choir. Then,

b. read **the text in the given rhythm**, repeating it as much as necessary until it is learned, depending on the complexity. Then:

c. Connect the rhythm with the melody and sing the piece without words, either on a vowel sound or on a separate syllable (la, la, la, or du, du, du). It is useful to combine **the melody and** rehearse the **rhythm without lyrics** in this way until the choir has mastered the piece thoroughly.

d. And only then **connect all three elements.** This method of work may seem boring and tedious, but experience shows that in this way you can save a lot of time, which in our working conditions is always precious.

5. The work on choral diction is critically important. As one famous choir conductor said, "Articulation, articulation, and again articulation!" The church choir is obliged to convey to the ears of the worshipers the liturgical text in the best possible way. You can't do it if you're barely opening your mouth or moving your tongue. There is nothing sadder than standing in the temple to hear an indistinct sound eruption from the choir, to the painfully familiar melody of the troparion of Tone 4, and at the same time not have a clue what the choir is singing about. This, unfortunately, is often observed. The late Archimandrite Matthew (Mormyl) noted that one of the differences between man and animal is his ability to make consonant sounds. Cats also make vowel sounds. Consonant sounds are characterized by the fact that

if the singers pronounce them exactly at the same time, they will be heard everywhere in the space, even if they are pronounced in a whisper. Therefore, the director must always take care to work toward clear choral diction.
6. When working on a piece at rehearsal, you should pay attention to the phrasing so that each part has a vocal line based on breathing, so that there is no ugly singing syllable-by-syllable, which is especially often observed in the performance of Obikhod chants.

And finally, in order for the singing in the church to be magnificent, that is, very beautiful (and everyone wants it to be just like that), the director and his singers need to have an understanding of the "culture of vocal sound." Unfortunately, this is rare. And yet, the overall sound of the choir largely depends on this. It is extremely important here that all members of a choral section form vowel sounds in the same way and sound as homogeneous as possible. If the director himself is a competent vocalist, then he must teach his choristers the correct sound production. Otherwise, a vocal teacher should be invited. Without this, the choir will not sound to its full potential. It is possible to correct the timbre variegation in the choral section by using appropriate vocal exercises to equalize the sound. To do this, the director must hear these faults. And in order to hear, he must learn to "listen." It should, unfortunately, be recognized that we rarely know how to "listen" these days.

As for intonation, it must be borne in mind that the errors here are twofold, either going flat or going sharp. As for going flat, it is natural and is caused by incorrect vocal technique, the incorrect breathing of the singers. We are all witnesses to how choirs drop a semitone or a tone, and sometimes one and a half, and this does not hurt the ear much, except for those who have perfect pitch. We take it quite calmly when the whole choir goes flat together without creating a noticeable cacophony. This defect can be cured by work on choral breathing and can be completely corrected. As for going sharp, it is much more difficult to correct it, because here the defect is not of technique, but of hearing, often congenital.

In any case, choir directors should know some basic principles from the field of vocal pedagogy so that they can teach their singers, but, unfortunately, this is extremely rare. You can't blame them for this, because most often their musical education is limited to a few years of lessons on the piano or some other instrument. And even that is not always the case. Unsurprisingly, their understanding of vocal science is most limited.

In a choral ensemble, in order to achieve unity, if you like, uniformity of sound, it is extremely important that all voices in a given part form the sound in the same way. Then, individual voices will not stand out and "stick out like a nail" from the general choral texture. Not only is the unity between the sections is important—unity between voices *within* the section is important as well. For example, let us imagine: there are 4 basses in a choir. On first glance, this seems to be a luxury. But this "luxury" has the following features: one sings with a trembling, but rather annoying, sharp sound. The second has a naturally good voice, but, on the other hand, sings with an artificially "darkened" timbre thrown back, apparently in order to sound "more bassy" in his mind, and he sings not like a "cello" but like a "drum," beating notes like one would a percussion instrument. The third emits continuous "white" sounds. The fourth is the only one who, in all conscience, can be called a "real bass," having the richest natural gift; however, being young, he imitates a hardened bass singer and, as a result, sings not with his natural sound, but a fake one, which is immediately obvious to the ear. Now go and make a single vocal section out of the four, which does not stand out from the choir, when they are not able to sing together with each other. In some amateur choirs, the following technique is used to achieve unity of sound: each part is assigned its own "leader," the most vocally fortunate singer, who leads the other weaker singers, who are instructed in turn to listen to the leader, and, if possible, merge with his sound. This technique, let's say, is somewhat controversial and is not used in professional choirs, but in amateur choirs, which is the majority of our church choirs, it is often beneficial.

§ 18
Notes of an Experienced Choir Director

In view of the fact that we are all different, and choir directors are different too, as a fresh look at the subject, I will allow myself to quote the notes of one experienced director on the method of conducting rehearsals.

Rehearsing:

Choir director's preparation:
- Master the content of the text.
- For new pieces, study and mark the score:
– melodies and repetitive motifs,
– keys and modulations,
– tempo and changes in it
– entrances and their indications,
– dynamics,
 – phrasing/breathing signs
– complex phrases that require special attention
– Learn every part
– Practice rehearsing the piece using good technique and expressive gestures
– Create a mental ideal for yourself – how do you imagine the sound?
- Plan your rehearsal
– Plan a sensible, effective rehearsal
– Think in advance how you will rehearse in order to achieve your ideal
– Dedicate the right amount of time for each piece
– Be prepared to be flexible!

Rehearsal:
- Start rehearsal on time.
- Let the choir warm up.
- Work through the most difficult passages while your choir is "fresh."
- Be picky about intonation, clean pick up and cut off, and a sense of ensemble.
- Review pieces learned in previous sessions.
- Move the rehearsal forward; don't lose the interest of your singers.

– Don't spend too much time on one phrase or on one piece.
– Don't stop the choir too often. When you repeat a piece, explain to a choir why you are doing it.
– Keep your remarks short. Sing more, talk less.
– Add a touch of humor from time to time.
- Praise and encourage your singers. Point out defects in a kind, positive manner.
- End the rehearsal on a positive note. Don't forget to thank the singers for their hard work.

- **Rehearsing new pieces:**

– Give a general overview of the piece: the text, its place in worship, the general mood, unique aspects, history, composer, etc.
– Learn the music. How much time you spend on this will depend on the ability of your singers.
– Give a verbal description of the melodies, phrasing, general sound, etc.
– Learn the piece in fragments, working backwards.
– Learn difficult rhythms by clapping your hands, or by speaking the words in the correct rhythm.
– Use the piano to work through difficult passages.
– If necessary, work on the vocal parts separately.
– Devote time to tuning chords and conveying an understanding of chord changes.
– When the choir is confident in the notes, work on the musicality, dynamics, phrasing, shades, balance, and sense of ensemble.
- After the first rehearsal, come back and study the score again – what points would you change now? What would you add to your performance?

§ 19
Difficulties with an Amateur Choir

The director of an amateur choir faces a difficult task that the conductors of professional choirs do not face. The latter do not need to spend time and effort on teaching the basics of vocal technique. They work with professionals who have passed a special audition and were selected by competition. In an amateur choir, the conductor, even if he has professional training, has to work with raw material. What complicates the work is that the process of singing requires a certain coordination, and this coordination often has to be taught and explained in abstract terms. You have to explain such concepts as: open sound, covered sound, support, mask, enlargement of vowels, and other similar terminology that usually is discussed only in a vocal studio.

Therefore, in order not to confuse the singers, it is not necessary to indulge in lengthy technical explanations – this is a waste of precious time – but to state everything in the simplest words. In this regard, the "Instruction to the Vocalist", dating back to the singing schools of Russian monasteries in the eighteenth century, can serve as a kind of guide for the choir. This humorous poem, which nevertheless contains useful serious recommendations for vocalists, touches on many facets of the art of singing. We present it in full:

Instruction to the Vocalist

To sing beautifully to the grave,
Make a dome from your palate,
Become hollow like a pipe,
And start singing from the forehead.

Feel two points:
In the stomach and in the head.
Push down on your stomach
And send the sound forward.

So as to sing and not to choke,
Don't forget to be surprised.
A short breath, like you're afraid,
Then pull on the sound like a string.

If you are going up,
You need to dig deeper.
Then you will yell louder than all,
Even if you have no voice with which to yell.

If you are going down,
Don't lose your head.
Don't growl like a beast,
"Open the door softly."

"Cover up the sound"
Is very difficult to explain.
To find a cover,
Add an "I" to "E."

An "A" - to "O", and "O" to "U,"
But not in the throat, but in the forehead.
And from the forehead to the belly
Only a sinking emptiness.

Sing softly, do not scream,
Silently learn the parts;
And don't listen to anyone,
Except for God alone.

§ 20
About "Tone-Deaf" Clergy

In speaking of "delight by the modulation of the chant," we touch upon the topic of church beauty and liturgical aesthetics. Here we are faced with the difficult question of how to be, how to act, how to rectify the situation, when a clergyman does not have a musical ear or is completely "tone deaf." In the old days, the absence of a musical ear was considered a barrier to ordination. But times have changed. Often, one of the following situations occurs:

1. The priest or deacon is what is called a monophone: having no ear whatsoever, he is guided by physical sensations and liturgizes always on one note that he finds most convenient. Once he has found this note, he stubbornly sticks to it. This, by the way, is not the worst case, since here there is a high chance of predictability and the choir director, knowing in advance which note the priest or deacon will intone, can adjust the tonality of the litany so as not to cause a harsh dissonance that would bother the congregation.

2. The priest or deacon has a limited ear. Sometimes he gets in tune with the choir and steadily holds that note. In other cases, he cannot come in on the right note. You can try to train such a cleric gradually as follows: the choir director adjusts the tonality of the choir to the note on which the cleric came in and supports it, thus avoiding a dissonance between the deacon and the choir. The deacon, having learned the "sweetness of hitting the right note," will instinctively strive towards it and will gradually "get it," that is, he will begin to serve in the tonality set by the director. But this is impossible in those cases when the choir director frantically clings on to his beloved "C, A, F" or "D, B, G" for the litanies and is not willing to part with them.

3. The priest or deacon is not musical at all to such an extent that he is completely unpredictable; during one litany he can change the pitch several times. He can usually survive a quick "Again and again ...", but things are much worse for longer litanies. Here the choir director is powerless, and the congregation is provided with an excellent opportunity to develop the virtue of patience.

§ 21
About Bell Ringing

Since the popular definition of the word music designates it as any organized sounds, our textbook would not be complete without a discussion of church bell ringing and its significance in church life, especially at the present time, when church life is developing more and more in our country and there is a whole a number of bell firms, where you can order whole sets of bells for your church. And where this issue is relevant, most often it has to be dealt with by the choir director. Therefore, we consider it appropriate, in order not to "reinvent the wheel", to place here two authoritative texts, the first from the well-known textbook on *The Law of God* by Archpriest Slobodsky, and the second from the book *Choral Singing* by N. Matveev (see appendix 12).

§ 22
Conclusion

Finally, a few general observations. Every church choir director should, first of all, be a churched person. Apart from other tasks, the choir director has one main goal: to be an Orthodox Christian, not only in words, but in lifestyle as well. He must truly be, not simply seem to be. Only with such a mental disposition will the director be able to cultivate in himself the church-liturgical instinct that will guide him in the direction of the choir in church. In that case, questions of tempo, dynamics, phrasing, and choice of repertoire will be decided on the basis of his spiritual quality, which will guarantee that nothing inappropriate and alien to the spirit of Orthodox worship will penetrate his choir. Then he will feel and provide that "sense of measure" in worship (meaning, "a sense of moderation"), in which there is nothing theatrical, emotional or vulgar – mistakes that even highly skilled musicians who "work" in the church often make. It is problematic when the choir director is "working" rather than "serving." This, unfortunately, also happens. Yet directing a choir is first and foremost a **ministry**, not a job, although much labor is required, and quite difficult labor at that. Therefore, the director must train himself to be not only a musician but also – and above all – a Christian. Raising one's general level of cultural refinement won't hurt, either. As the saying goes, *noblesse oblige*.

Appendix 1:

The Bakhmetev Obikhod Title Page

Appendix 2:
Bakhmetev Obikhod sample page

Appendix 3:

Dogmatic Theotokia in the eight tones, Znamenny chant (square notation)

Appendix 4:

Cheat Sheet

	TROPARION / KONTAKION	STICHERA	IRMOS	PROKIMENON
Tone 1				
Tone 2				
Tone 3				
Tone 4				
Tone 5				
Tone 6				
Tone 7				
Tone 8				

"CHEAT SHEET" SUGGESTED

	Tone 1	Tone 2	Tone 3	Tone 4	Tone 5	Tone 6	Tone 7	Tone 8
Troparion/ Kontakion (Sunday Resurrectional Troparia)	When the Stone had been sealed by the Jews	When Thou didst descend unto life immortal	Let the Heavens rejoice, let earthly things be glad	Having heard the joyful proclamation from the angel	Let us, O Faithful, praise and worship the Word	Angelic hosts were above Thy tomb, and they that guarded Thee became as dead	Thou didst destroy death by Thy Cross	From on high didst Thou descend, O Compassionate One
Stichera (Dogmatic Theotokia)	Let us hymn the Virgin Mary,/ the glory of the whole world	The shadow of the law passed away when grace arrived/ For, as the bush wrapped in flame did not burn	How can we not marvel at they giving birth/ To the God-man,/ O all ho-noured one.	The Prophet David/ The forefather of God/ For thy sake gaveth voice beforehand in psalmody concerning Thee	Once, the image of the Bride who knoweth not wedlock was inscribed in the Red Sea/ There Moses was the parter of the wa-ters	Who doth not call thee blessed,/ O all-holy Virgin	Thou hast been known to have become a Mother in supernatural manner, appeared on earth and dwelt among men!/ For He Who Virgin in manner past recounting and received flesh from the pure Virgin	In his love for mankind, the King of Heaven appeared on earth and dwelt among men!/ When there with, he smote the sea/
Prokeimenon (Sunday Liturgy Prokeimena)	Let Thy mercy, O Lord, be upon us, as we have set our hope on Thee	The Lord is my strength and my song, He hath become my salvation	Sing praises to our God sing praises/ Sing praises to our King, sing praises	How magnified are Thy works, O Lord,/ in wisdom hast Thou made them all	Thou, O Lord, shalt protect us and preserve us from this generation for ever	O Lord save Thy people and bless Thine inheritance	The Lord shall give strength to his people, the Lord will bless his people with peace.	Pray and make your vows before the Lord, our God
Irmois (Saturday-Night Vigil)	In God-like wise hath Thy victorious right arm/ Been glorified in strength	In the deep aforetime did the overwhelming force overthrow all the host of pharaoh/	He who of old by his gesture divine/ Had passed through the red sea's abyss with foot unwet	When Israel of old/ Didst Christ cast into the Red Sea	The horse and its rider/ passed on foot over the deep as it had been dry land/	When Israel passed on foot over the deep as it had been dry land/	At my nod, O Lord/ The nature of waters which hitherto had flowed freely/	The wonderworking Rod of Moses aforetime/ When there with, he smote the sea/

APPENDIX 4: "CHEAT SHEET"

Appendix 5:

Podobny/Automela

Tone I
Joy of the Ranks of Heaven

6 strophes: A B A B A C

(musical notation with lyrics:)

Joy of the ranks of hea- ven, mighty interces-sion for men on earth, O all-pure Vir- gin: Save us who have re- course un- to thee; for af- ter God it is up- on thee that we have set our hope, O The- o- to- kos.

Automelon "Joy of the ranks of heaven..."
Source: Octoechos, Tone I, Sunday evening, theotokion for aposticha stichera.
Pattern: ABABAC (6 strophes)
Sample Texts:

Thou art the first among the incorporeal angels, the minister of God's divine radiance, a beholder and initiate of the mystery, O Michael, supreme commander: save us that piously honor thee each year and hymn the Trinity with faith.

O Michael, chief commander, with fear we hymn thee as first captain of the heavenly ranks, mighty intercessor, protector and deliverer of men on earth: and we pray that thou deliver us from every deadly pestilence.

As chief captain of the divine hosts of heaven thou dost today summon the choirs of men to hold one radiant festival with the angels, that of their divine synaxis, and with them to chant the thrice-holy hymn unto God.

O Michael, divine intellect, do thou keep and protect all throughout life us that with faith flee beneath the shelter of thy divine pinions; and at the dreaded hour of our death, O archangel, do thou stand forth as a most gracious helper for us all.

All of us, the multitudes of the pious, celebrating the sacred feast now with joy, exclaim with loud voices, faithfully praising the brother of God, the disciple of the Lord, in psalms and hymnody; for he ever prayeth that we be saved.

Thou wast shown to be the Lord's brother in the flesh by His own desire, O wise one, His disciple and an eye-witness to divine mysteries, having fled with Him to Egypt, with Joseph and the Mother of Jesus. With them pray that we be saved.

The choir of the apostles chose thee to be the first bishop in holy Sion for Christ our Benefactor, in that thou art His kinsman and brother according to the flesh, His companion and the heir to His footsteps, O James.

Let us all praise King David, the ancestor of God for from him sprang forth the rod of the Virgin, and from her blossomed the Flower, even Christ, Who hath called forth Adam and Eve from corruption, in that He is full of lovingkindness.

In old age Joseph the betrothed beheld the things foretold by the prophets clearly fulfilled, having received a strange betrothal and a revelation from angels that cry, Glory to God, Who hath sent down peace upon the earth!

Appendix 5

Tone II
O House of Ephratha

5 strophes: A B C D E

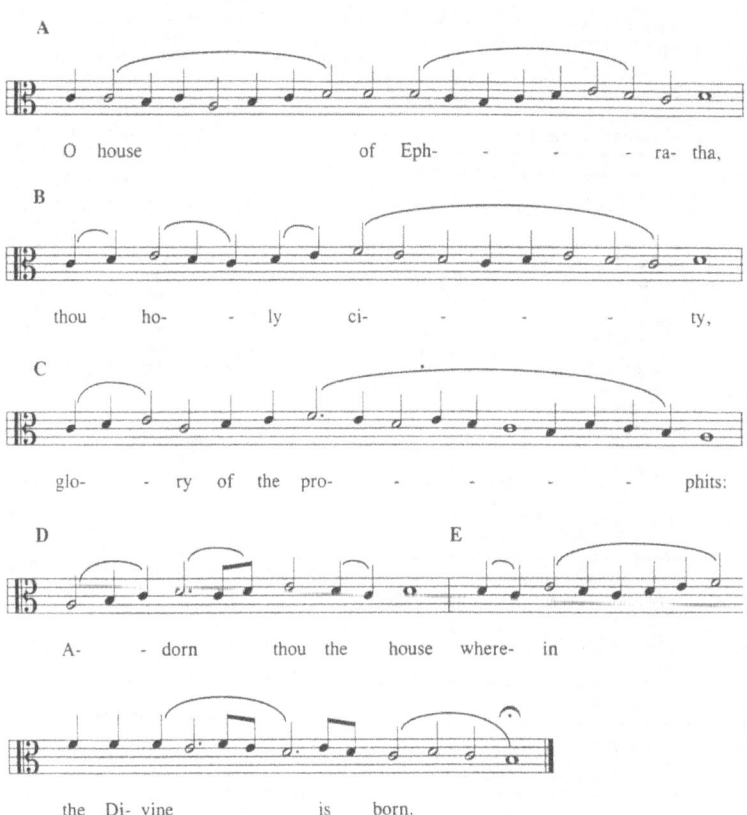

Automelon "O house of Ephratha ... "
Source: Menaion, Sunday before the Nativity of Christ, 1st sticheron of the aposticha, but only when this Sunday falls on December 24th.
Pattern: ABCDE (5 strophes)
Sample Texts:
    Christ cometh * to crush the evil one, * to enlighten those in darkness, * and to loose those in bond s. * Let us go forth to meet Him!

Dance, O Sion! * Adorn thyself well, O cave! * Make ready, O Bethlehem! * For, lo! the Virgin cometh * to give birth unto the Christ!

Sing praise and glory, * ye nations of the gentiles! * Ye magi, make haste in earnest, * bearing gifts, * while the shepherds pipe.

From thine earliest infancy * wast thou shown to be * a sanctified vessel * and the abode of the all-holy Spirit, * O our God-bearing father.

Bearing upon thy shoulders* the Cross of the Lord,* O Sabbas, our father, * thou didst utterly lay waste * to demonic fantasies.

Having renounced the deception of the evil demons * by the power of the Cross, * thou didst shine forth * the glory of Christ, * O Sabbas, our father.

In the streams of the Jordan * hast Thou appeared, * O Effulgence of the glory of the Father, * washing away by baptism* the defilement of our souls.

O prophet John,* receive thou the Deliverer of the world* Who cometh like a servant,* and baptize the Creator* for the renewal of mortals.

Enlightenment is come!* Deliverance hath appeared!* Come ye to the Jordan,* and let us descend together to be cleansed * and to sing the hymns of the forefeast!

A great and awesome mystery * is now accomplished: * for the Master of all * is baptized at the hand of His servant * for the purification of all men.

From on high * the Father cried aloud: * "This is my beloved Son * Who is now baptized in the flesh* in the waters of the Jordan!"

The ranks of angels,* beholding the Master,* in the guise of a servant,* baptized in the waters,* were amazed and chanted.

The Effulgence of the Father's glory * hath appeared * in the streams of the Jordan, * washing away through baptism * the defilement of our souls.

Receive as a servant * the Deliverer of the world, * O prophet John, * and baptize the Creator, * unto the restoration of men.

Appendix 5

<u>Tone II</u>
When from the Tree

9 strophes: A B C D A B C D E

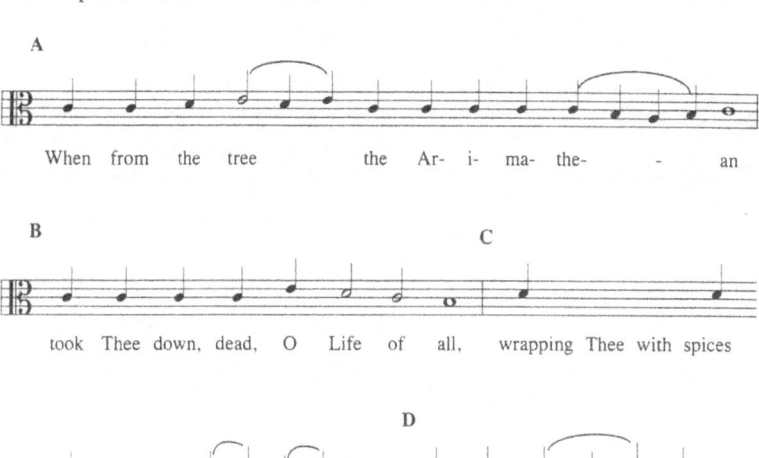

A
When from the tree the Ar- i- ma- the- - an

B
took Thee down, dead, O Life of all,

C
wrapping Thee with spices

D
in a winding sheet, O Christ, he was moved by love

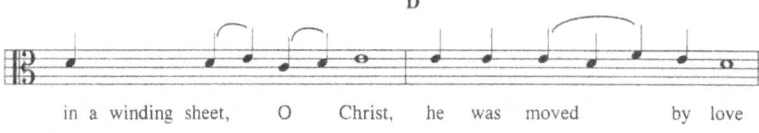

A
to kiss Thine incorrupt bo- - dy

B
with his heart and lips.

C
Yet, beset by fear he cried unto Thee re- joi- - cing:

D
Glo- ry to

E
Thy con- de- cen- - sion, O Thou who lo- vest man- kind.

Automelon   "When from the Tree..."
Source: Lenten Triodion, Good Friday vespers, 1st sticheron of the aposticha.
Pattern: ABCD ABCD E   (9 strophes)
Sample Texts:

When the ice of ignorance beset all creation with hostile assault and a multitude of idols were worshipped, then, O glorious martyrs, ye abolished this with zealous heart and the fervor of divine faith; and ye manifestly shed your blood with love for Him Who shed His blood on the Cross.

When, at God's behest, ye set yourselves apart for supernatural struggles, ignoring your corruptible bodies, then, strengthened by the power of the Most High, ye were undaunted by the fire or the cutting sword. Wherefore, bending your necks before God, O blessed ones, ye accepted death with joy.

O valiant athlete Peon, Valerian, Chariton and Charita, O godly Justin, Euelpistus and glorious Hierax, who dyed your vesture in your divine blood and have arrayed yourselves therein together, with the angels ye stand before Christ the King and Master of all in the heavens.

When thou didst wound thy soul with divine desire, O most blessed one, rejoicing thou didst take up thy cross and follow after Christ; and having mortified the wisdom of the flesh through abstinence, thou didst receive the living activity of the Spirit, enabling thee to banish the winter of infirmities with the fervor of thy right acceptable prayers. Wherefore, together we bless thee.

When thou didst cleanse the sight of thy soul through earnest prayers and most steadfast fasting, O father, thou didst become a temple of the three-sunned Godhead; and, receiving the divine anointing of the priesthood of God, thou didst enter within things inaccessible, offering up in sacrifice Him that was slain for thy sake, for the sake of an ineffable companionship.

Manifest as meek and guileless, O father Theoctistus, in wholeness of character didst thou truly inherit the land of the meek; and deified through communion with God, thou dost delight in the sustenance of true joy and gladness. Cease thou not to remember us here that ardently honor thee and celebrate thy godly repose.

Appendix 5

<u>Tone IV</u>
As One Valiant Among the Martyrs

9 strophes: A B C D E F G H I

As one val- iant among the mar- tyrs, O pas- sion bear- er George, we praise thee, as- semb- ling to- day; for hav- ing fin- ished the race, thou didst keep the faith, and hast re- ceived from God a crown for thy vic- t'ry.

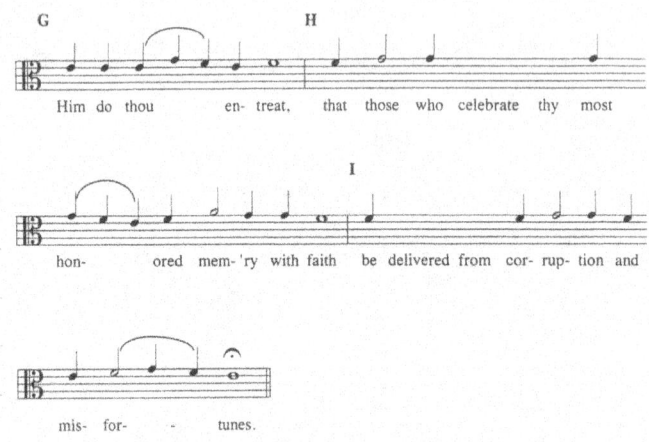

Automelon "As one valiant among the martyrs..."
Source: Menaion, April 23 (feast of St. George), Great Vespers, 1st sticheron for "Lord, I have cried..."
Pattern: ABCDEFGHI (nine strophes)
Sample Texts:

The honored temple maketh ready * to receive within itself * the Lord Who cometh as a Babe * and noetically illumineth with grace * His most faithful assembly beloved of God; * wherefore it crieth out: * "Thou art the glory, the boast * and the adornment of my fullness, * O Word Who becamest a Babe in the flesh for my sake!"

The most splendid bridal-chamber, * the all-precious tabernacle, * the holy and spacious temple, * bearing the Lord within the chambers of the temple, * doth betroth herself beforehand to His honored Church * and ever prayeth, * that those who unceasingly glorify her * as the true Theotokos * be delivered from corruption and misfortunes.

Let us now offer unto Christ * the praise of the forefeast, * glorifying His condescension; * for, carried in the Virgin's arms * as an infant, * He cometh to lie in the arms of Symeon, * crying out to all men, * and to deify their nature, * as Benefactor and Lord.

Let us bless Nicholas, the most glorious hierarch, the star unwaning of the all-radiant Sun, the spiritual noetic heaven which showeth forth the saving glory of God, the divine preacher, the enlightener of the heathen, the river flowing with the waters of knowledge, watering the hearts of the faithful.

Thy passage was by sea from Myra in Lycia to the city of Bari, O hierarch; for, with the permission of the Master of all, thy coffin was taken from thy grave by a monk who piously served at thy tomb and rendered thee honor; and it passed from the East unto the West, O Nicholas most glorious.

Having sanctified the waters of the sea by thy voyage to the city of Bari, thou didst pour forth myrrh, O glorious one, healing incurable sufferings. Thou becamest its refuge, defender and deliverer, O hierarch Nicholas, praying to the Savior and King of all.

By thy fiery teachings is all the tinder of heresy utterly consumed, O all-glorious one; and by the abyss of thine understandings is the wicked army of the unruly drowned, O venerable Athanasius. And the Church of the faithful is adorned every day by thy doctrines, O blessed one, and doth honor thee, crying aloud.

Appendix 5

TONE V
"REJOICE, THOU LIFE-BEARING CROSS..."

14 strophes: ABCD ABCD ABCD A E

Re - joice, thou Life - bear -ing Cross,   in - vin - ci - ble vic - t'ry of

pi - - - e - ty,   door to pa - ra - dise,   con - firm - a - tion of the

faith - - ful,   ram - part of the Church,   where- by cor - rup - tion hath

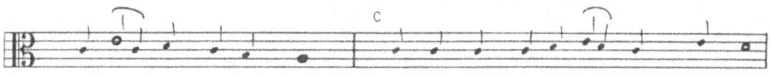
been ut - ter - ly des - troyed,   the dom - in - ion of death tram - pled down,

and we have been lift - ed up from earth to those who are in hea - - - ven,

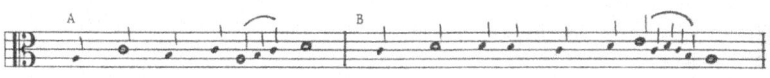
in - vin - ci - ble wea - pon,   con - tend - er a - gainst the de - - mons,

Automelon "Rejoice,..."
Source: Menaion, September 15 (Afterfeast of the Exaltation of the Cross), 1st sticheron on "Lord, I have cried..."
Pattern: ABCD ABCD ABCD A E (14 strophes)
Sample Texts:

Rejoice, O Cross of the Lord, whereby mankind hath been released from the curse, thou ensign of joy, who in thine exaltation drivest away the enemy, O most honored one, our helper, dominion of kings, might of the righteous, splendor of priests, who, when traced, dost deliver from evils, staff of power, whereby we are shepherded, weapon of peace around whom the angels stand in fear, divine glory of Christ, Who granteth the world great mercy!

Rejoice, O guide of the blind, physician of the ailing, resurrection of all the dead, who hast lifted us up who have fallen into corruption, O precious Cross, whereby the curse hath been annulled and incorruption hath blossomed forth, and we mortals have been deified, and the devil hath been utterly cast down! Beholding thee today uplifted in the arms of the hierarch, we exalt Him Who was lifted up upon thee, and we bow down before thee, richly drawing forth great mercy.

Rejoice, truly fragrant vessel of the struggles of fasting; for, having taken thy cross upon thy shoulder and offered thyself to Christ the Master, O most blessed one, thou didst trample down the base understanding of the flesh, didst illumine thy soul with the virtues, and didst take flight to divine desire. Wherefore, surrounding thy most holy shrine, O all-lauded Sabbas, we ask that, by thy supplications, we may receive God's love for mankind, and that the world be granted great mercy.

O God-bearing Sabbas, having drawn nigh unto the fire of the Spirit, thou hast shown thyself forth as a divinely radiant ember, enlightening the souls of those who have recourse to thee in faith, O thou of godly wisdom, leading them to the never-waning Light, O venerable one. And, bedewed from on high with grace divine, thou didst quench the burning coal of the desert. Wherefore, Christ, the Helmsman of divine righteousness, hath manifestly bestowed upon thee a crown of victory, O blessed one. Him do thou entreat, that He grant our souls great mercy.

Tone VI
On the Third Day

6 strophes: A B A B A var. C

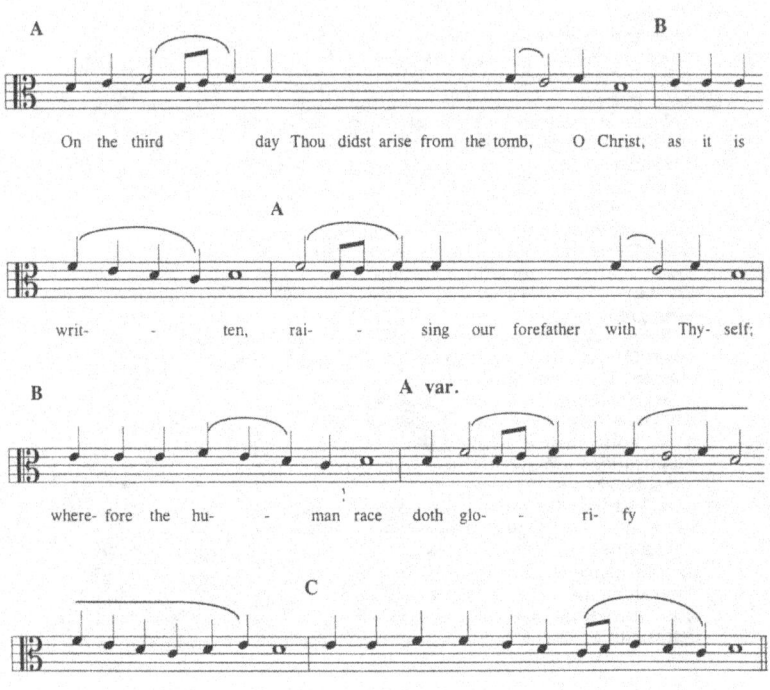

Automelon   "On the third day..."
Source: Octoechos, Tone VI, Sunday matins, 4th sticheron of the Praises.
Pattern: ABABA(var.)C
Sample Texts:

    The angelic hosts, O Christ, which stand before Thy throne, pray for the human race. Wherefore, at their entreaties, do Thou cast down the audacity of the pagans, giving peace unto all the faithful.

    O ye ranks of angels, that ever hold chorus about the throne of the King of all: preserve us that with faith call upon you, and deliver us all from torment.

    An awesome mystery do I behold! For God Who holdeth all creation in the palm of His hand is surrounded in the flesh in a manger of dumb beasts, and He is wrapped in rags Who clotheth the sea in darkness.

    Our incorporeal God becometh incarnate! He Who is without beginning taketh on a beginning! He Who is full now emptieth Himself through the Virgin in a little cave! And He Who nurtureth every creature is nurtured on milk as a babe.

    Shepherds dance at Thy nativity and offer up glory with the angels; the star offereth a gift, and magi pay homage; and men, saved, magnify the Theotokos.

    O blessed Nicholas, have pity on me who fall down before thee, I pray, and enlighten the eyes of my soul, O all-wise one, that in purity I may gaze upon the compassionate Bestower of light.

    As thou hast boldness before God, O most blessed hierarch Nicholas, rescue me from the enemies who seek to do me evil, and save me from men of blood, O holy one.

    O hierarch, we, the faithful, have acquired thee as a haven unbeset by storms, an impregnable rampart, a tower of confirmation and a portal of repentance, a guide and champion of our souls.

    A stranger to the world, yet not estranging thyself from those therein, taking pity on the people, though called a fool, thou instructest in wisdom, and, showing all manner of endurance, thou healest the suffering; for the power of Christ is made perfect in thy weakness.

    Thou didst give away thine earthly wealth, O Xenia, as it were something unrighteous. And thou didst spurn the shelter of thy home, covering thyself with the mercy of God. And, emulating the wandering of Christ, thou hast attained unto the kingdom of Christ.

Having placed all their hope

Tone VI

Strophes: A B |:C D E:| F

A Hav- ing placed all their hope in the hea- vens, B the saints laid up
C for themselves a trea- sure which can- not be sto- len a- way;
D they free- ly re- ceived E and free- ly give hea-ling to the in- firm.
C fol- low- ing the Gos- pel, D they acquired neither sil- ver
E nor gold, but be- stowed be- ne- fac- tions up- on C
D both men and beasts, that, ob- ed- i- ent to Christ,
E they might pray with bold- ness F in be- half of our souls.

Automelon "Having set all their hope..."
Source: Menaion, November 1 (feast of Sts. Cosmas & Damian), 1st sticheron on "Lord, I have cried..."
Pattern: AB |: CDE :| F (11 strophes, or approximately so)
Sample Texts:

The never-setting Sun doth come to shine forth from the Virgin's womb and to enlighten all the world. Let us make haste to meet Him with pure eyes and deeds; and let us now make ready in spirit to receive Him that cometh into His own through a strange birth, as He hath been well pleased to do, that, as He is compassionate, He might lead us up that have estranged ourselves from the life of Eden, and might be born in Bethlehem.

God the Word, Who is upborne upon the shoulders of the cherubim, having united Himself hypostatically to the flesh, hath made His abode within the womb of the all-immaculate one and become a man; and He hath come to earth to be born of the tribe of Judah. The holy cave is beautifully adorned, like a most magnificent palace, for the King of all; and the manger, wherein the Virgin Mary layeth the Infinite One like a babe, is like a fiery throne, and serveth for the renewal of creation.

Unto the ends of the earth hath the memory of the forefathers been manifest as truly filled with light and shining with rays of grace; for Christ, the radiant Sun, shining from afar on high, doth lead forth an assembly of stars which shineth with Him, and in the midst of Bethlehem a nativity is shown to be that of God and man. Therefore, piously clapping our hands, with faith let us all join chorus to utter pre-festive praise unto His nativity.

Rejoicing today, Adam is adorned with the glory of divine communion, as the foundation and confirmation of the wise forefathers; and with him Abel doth leap for joy and Enoch is glad, and Seth danceth together with Noah; the all-praised Abraham doth chant with the patriarchs, and from on high Melchizedek doth behold a birth wherein a father had no part. Wherefore, celebrating the divine memory of the forefathers of Christ, we beseech Him, that our souls be saved.

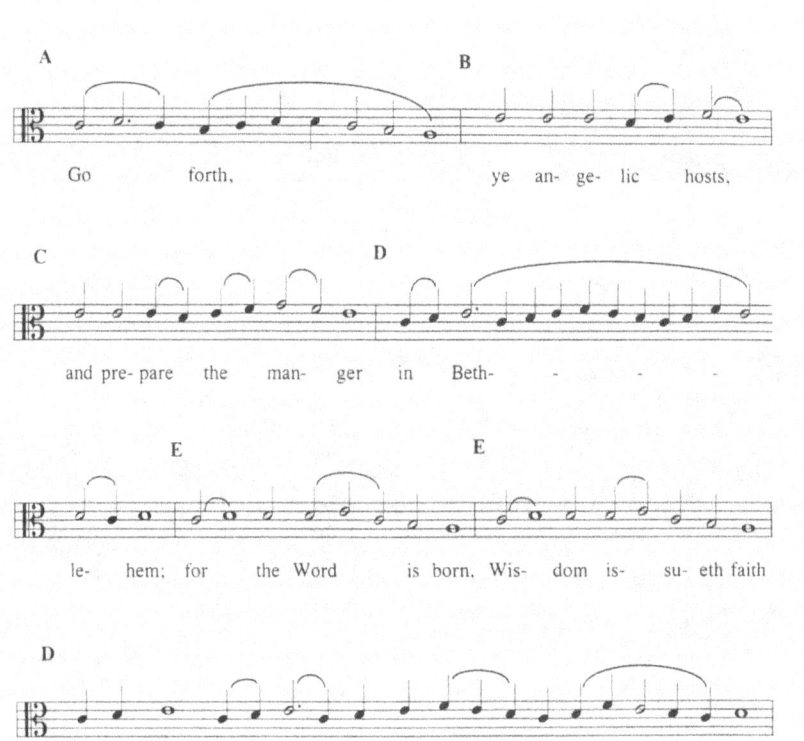

Appendix 5

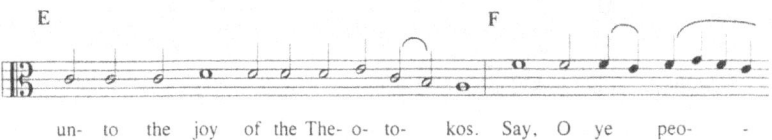
un- to the joy of the The- o- to- kos. Say, O ye peo-

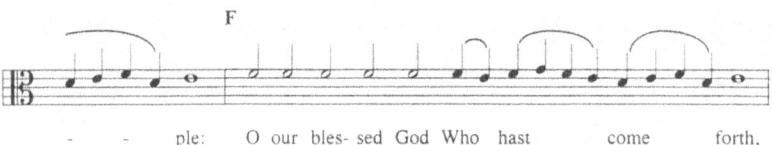
- - ple: O our bles- sed God Who hast come forth,

glo- - ry be to Thee!

Automelon "Come forth, ye angelic hosts..."
Source: Menaion, December 20 (forefeast of the Nativity of Christ), 1st sticheron of the Praises.
Pattern: ABCDEEDEFFG (11 strophes)
Sample Texts:

Now are the ancient manifestations resolved: for a Virgin hath conceived in her womb; for the Stone hath been cut from the mountain, the rod of Jesse hath sprouted forth, and the dew of Gideon hath now been poured forth upon the earth. O ye people, let us cry out: Christ, the King of Israel, cometh forth!

Now are strange aspects of a strange birthgiving seen. How doth He Who sitteth with the Father in the highest desire to be laid in a manger of dumb beasts? How is He Whom no one can touch wrapped in swaddling-clothes? How is He Who is everywhere present contained in a cave? Ye people, let us cry out: Christ, the King of Israel, cometh forth!

He Who worketh miracles, smiting Egypt with plagues and raining manna down upon His foolish people, is incarnate and nurtured with milk. And, seen as a babe, He fleeth the tyrant Herod, borne by His Virgin Mother, as upon a cloud, as Isaiah of most godly sight foresaw.

The Child Who hath been King from before time began is born of His own will! A Son hath been given us! Hearken, ye nations! Pay heed, O Israel! Understand and submit yourselves! For He is with us Who will grind down and wipe from the earth every kingdom and principality which hath not obeyed Him!

All creation riseth with joy to meet the feast, and the heavens rejoice with us; for, the Creator, incarnate of the Virgin, hath most gloriously been seen in a manger in Bethlehem of Judah. Let us say to the people, O our blessed God, Who hast been born, glory be to Thee!

Being the pre-eternal Word, Thou camest to earth to become incarnate of the Virgin, and wast seen as a Babe, that Thou mightest make mortals heavenly. Wise men didst Thou bring from Persia to worship Thee, O Compassionate One; and with them we cry out in joy, O our blessed God, Who hast been born, glory be to Thee!

O Jesus, Who for our sake shone forth from the Father before the ages, for our sake Thou didst appear as a little Babe, wishing to renew all men, who had grown old through the transgression. Wherefore, in thanksgiving we all ever cry out to Thee, O our blessed God, Who hast been born, glory be to Thee!

Appendix 5

TONE VIII

"O ALL-GLORIOUS WONDER..."

9 strophes: ABABCDABE

O all glo-ri-ous won--der! The Life-bear-ing Tree, The all-

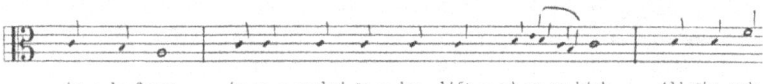
ho-ly Cross, is re-vealed to-day, lift-ed up on high. All the ends

of the earth glo-ri-fy it, and the hordes of the de-mons are af-flict-

ed. O what a gift hath been giv-en to mor--tals! There-by, O Christ,

save Thou our souls, in that Thou a-lone art com-pas--sion-ate.

Automelon "O all-glorious wonder..."
Source: Menaion, September 14 (Exaltation of the Cross), 1st sticheron of the Praises
Pattern: ABABCDABE (9 strophes)
Sample Texts:

O most glorious wonder! O providence divine! A most precious treasure, hidden beneath the earth to preserve it from mockery, is discovered in the fullness of time: for lo! the holy relics of the martyred king are revealed as a new and much-healing well-spring for all who with faith bow down before them and glorify God Who is wondrous in His saints.

O wondrous solemnity! O most joyous feast! For we celebrate the most splendid memorial of Edward the King, the merciful healer of the afflicted and the diseased, the defender of the orphaned, the consoler of the grieving, uprooter of irreverence and planter of piety, the bold intercessor and advocate for our souls.

O the richness of the great wisdom of God! O the providence of God! The holy relics of the martyred Orthodox king are entrusted to the Orthodox Church! Wherefore, let us now bow down with faith, invoking the crowned passion-bearer in prayer; and let us fervently offer thanksgiving unto Christ God Who hath given us such a treasure and doth ever show forth His mercy upon us.

Blessed is the Monastery of Sarov, which hath thee, O venerable father Seraphim, as a treasury of virtues, a vessel of purity and chastity, a receptacle of grace, a fount of healings, a physician who cureth the infirm without fee, a true faster, a comforter of the afflicted, and a calm haven for them that are tempest-tossed by the passions of life. O venerable father Seraphim, pray that peace and great mercy be granted unto us who keep thine honored memory.

O blessed Xenia, loving the heavenly homeland, thou didst truly abide on earth as a stranger, passing through it as though it were a foreign land. And now, abiding in the house of the heavenly Father, and delighting in the hospitality of the Master in the mansions on high, forget not those who with faith celebrate thy memory, and deliver us from multifarious tribulations, remembering us before the throne of the Lord of glory.

O glorious Xenia, like a wise virgin thou didst go forth to meet Christ, the Bridegroom, at the midnight of thy life, bearing a lamp alight with the flame of divine love, and though called a fool by the world, thou art full of transcendent wisdom. Wherefore, unto us who celebrate thy memory with faith give thou of the oil of wisdom which thou hast acquired in abundance, pouring forth drops thereof onto our wounds.

An Extract from Bishop Alypy's Grammar of the Church Slavonic Language

The Versification of Liturgical Hymns

Liturgical hymns -- stichera, troparia, kontakia, etc. -- are meant to be chanted, as is borne witness to even by their very superscriptions, which indicate that one or another tone is appointed for them.

Just as chant has its system, so does hymnography.

Ecclesiastical chants are distributed through eight tones (echos), which comprise the system of the octoechos. At the present time we take the eight tones as eight particular melodies; but originally they had a somewhat different meaning: the tone signified a given fret, as on a lyre, and later indicated a scale with intervals variously placed (the modern scale is called a gamut). The melodies of the hymns were composed in these eight scales just as they are now composed in basically two scales -- the major and the minor -- when we borrow from or imitate "general music". Each fret/tone, besides the basic significance of scale, was complicated yet further by certain melodic peculiarities.

In the beginning, every hymn had its own melody. The ancient hymnographers were also chanters, and simultaneously composed both words and melody. Later, they began to compose hymns without particular melodies, to be executed according to the melody of another hymn known to the chanters. Thus, two types of hymn appeared: hymns with independent melodies began to be called idiomela, and hymns with borrowed melodies were called prosomia. For ease of execution, the prosomia must repeat the syllabic arrangement of the hymn exactly, i.e., the arrangement of accented and unaccented syllables in its model. In such a case the model is referred to as the automelon. Such a correspondence between the automelon and the prosomia is preserved only in the original Greek texts: in the process of translation into another language,... it, of necessity, disappears. The mass of prosomia are identified by the name (the initial words) of the automelon to whose melody they are chanted.

An example of the syllabic relationship between prosomia in the Greek text follows:

Πρὸς τὸ Οἶκος τοῦ Εὐφραθᾶ. (ПОДОБЕНЪ: Доме Єѵфраѳовъ:)

1) Πάντες τῇν τῶν σεπτῶν (6 syllables)
2) νῦν προπατόρων μνήμην (7)
3) τελέσωμεν, ὑμνοῦντες (7)
4) τήν τούτων πολιτείαν (7)
5) δι᾽ ἧς ἐμεγαλύνθησαν (8)

Всѣ честныхъ
нынѣ праотецъ память
совершающихъ поющіе
боугодное ихъ житіе,
єгоже ради возвеличишаса.

-2-

1) Ἔσβεσαν τοῦ πυρὸς (6)   ѹ̈гасиша ѻ҆гненнꙋю
2) τὴν δύναμιν οἱ παῖδες (7)   силꙋ ѻ҆троцы,
3) χορεύοντες ἐν μέσῳ (7)   ликꙋюще посредѣ
4) καμίνου καὶ ὑμνοῦντες (7)   пещи, и҆ поюще
5) Θεὸν τὸν παντοδύναμον (8)   бга всесильнаго.

1) Λάκκῳ κατακλεισθείς. (6)   Въ ровѣ заключннъ,
2) θηροὶ συνῳκιομένος (7)   sвѣремъ сѡбитатель,
3) Δανιὴλ ὁ προφήτης (7)   данїилъ пррокъ,
4) ἀμέτοχος τῆς τούτων (7)   непричастенъ сихъ
5) ἐδείκνυτο κακώσεως (8)   показася ѡ҆ѕлобленїа.

    The following is a schematic of the metric arrangement of the syllables in the above prosomia:

1) ′ ∪ ∪ ∪ ∪ ′
2) ∪ ′ ∪ ∪ ∪ ′ ∪
3) ∪ ∪ ′ ∪ ∪ ′ ∪
4) ∪ ′ ∪ ∪ ∪ ′ ∪
5) ∪ ′ ∪ ∪ ∪ ′ ∪ ∪

(The prosomia are taken from the service for the Sunday of the Holy Forefathers)

    As is obvious from the examples cited, the accented and unaccented syllabels within a given prosomion have no meter at all: they acquire significance only in connection with other prosomia, i.e. the first line of one prosomion corresponds in the arrangements of its syllables to the first line of any other, as do the lines following. Syllables which have a definite place in all prosomia are those with fundamental accents; the rest of the accented syllables are equivalent to unaccented syllables. One may call such a syllabic system of prosomia a parallelism between syllables and tone, for the verses of the prosomia parallel the verses of the automelon. The ease of such a system is particularly apparent when the melody is complicated....

    Ancient Russian chant was composed according to a single scale, and the difference of tones lay in the fact that each tone possessed its own melodic peculiarities (ultimate and penulatimate sounds, melodic phrases, etc.).

    In view of the fact that there is no syllabic correspondence between the automelon and the prosomia in the Church Slavonic text, the melody of the automelon must be adapted to each prosomion in accordance with a somewhat different syllabic pattern, i.e. when there are not enough syllables, more notes are chanted on a single syllable, and when there extra syllables, they are

Appendix 5   109

-3-

chanted in "recitative" on a single note.

In Russian chant, when <u>prosomia</u> are executed, certain melodies require a set number of phrases if one is to conclude the piece properly. For example, when executing the <u>prosomion</u> "O all-glorious wonder..." according to the melody given in <u>The Chanters' Companion</u>, the <u>prosomion</u> must be divided into nine phrases. Other <u>prosomion</u> melodies are more flexible, permitting the chanters to reach the end of the hymn after any number of phrases....

The following example represents an attempt at achieving parallelism in both syllable arrangement and melody in a Church Slavonic text.

The <u>automelon</u> "O marvellous wonder..." (the first sticheron on "Lord, I have cried..." from the service of the Dormition of the Theotokos), and a <u>prosomion</u> sticheron from the service of the Venerable Alypius (composed by the author; from "Lord, I have cried..." from the service of the saint for August 17th):

-4-

From the above-outlined system of _automela_ and _prosomia_ it is apparent that the _prosomia_ constitute a certain simplification in chant; thus, the weekday services are composed almost exclusively of _prosomia_, and the typicon's expression "if their be an _idiomelon_" serves as a certain sign of festivity. Sunday services and services of the greater feasts are, for the most part, composed of _idiomela_.

Contemporary tones/melodies in Russian ecclesiastican singing represent the fruit of a further simplification of ecclesiastical chant. These are _prosomia_ of a sort too, suitable for chanting with any number of syllables and with any number of phrases, and they are thus quite easy for chanters who do not know the genuine melodies of the _automela_ and _prosomia_.

Canons also are composed (in the Greek text) according to the above-detailed syllabic system. The irmos comprises a sort of _automelon_, and the troparia of the canon imitate the syllabic arrangement of the irmos.

The akathis hymn to the Mother of God, which is chanted in Great Lent on the feast of the Laudation, is similarly composed. All the ikoi and kontakia are patterned after the syllabic arrangement of Ikos I and Kontakion II. Kontakion I is a separate case, like an _idiomelon_.

The metric measure of classical antiquity was not made use of in the composition of the Church's services, apparently because the difference in vowel length had already disappeared by the Byzantine period, and any attempt to execute it would have presented gret difficulties. However, there are a few cases where classic meter is employed. Iambic hexameter is used in the second canons for the feasts of the Nativity of Christ, the Theophany and Pentecost....

Translated from Bishop Alypy's _Grammar of the Church Slavonic Language_ (Jordanville, N.Y.: St. Job of Pochaev Press, 1984), pp. 253-257. Isaac Lambertsen, translator.

Appendix 6:

The Eight Tones – Monophonic Obikhod

THE EIGHT TONES

Musical Notes for the Sunday Octoechos

Appendix 6

Appendix 6

Appendix 6

Appendix 6   129

Appendix 6

Sunday Troparia and Kontakia

Troparion, Seventh Tone, continued

to pro-claim that Thou didst a-rise, O Christ God, and grantest to the world great mer-cy.

Kontakion:

No long-er will the dominion of death be able to keep men cap-tive; for Christ hath descended, demolishing and de-stroying the pow-ers there-of. Ha-des is bound; the prophets rejoice with one voice, say-ing: A Sav-iour hath come for them that have faith. Come forth, ye faith-ful, for the Res-ur-rec-tion.

EIGHTH TONE:

God is the Lord and hath ap-peared un-to us. Bless-ed is He

Appendix 6

Tone One, continued

Ode 4:

Having per-ceived thee with his proph-et-ic eyes as a moun-tain over-shadowed by di-vine grace, Abbacum foretold that out of thee would come the Holy One of Is-ra-el for our sal-va-tion and re-fash-ion-ing.

Ode 5:

O Thou Who hast en-light-ened us with the brightness of Thy com-ing, O Christ, and hast il-lumined the ends of the world with Thy Cross; Enlighten with the light of di-vine knowl-edge the hearts of them that right-ly praise Thee.

Ode 6:

The lowest a-byss hath en-com-passed us, and there is none

Appendix 6   135

24   The Eirmosi Tones

First Tone, Ode 6, continued

to de=liv-er us.   We are counted as sheep for the slaugh-ter.

Save Thy people, O our God;   for Thou art the strength of

the weak,   and the   a-mend-ment.

Ode 7:

We faith-ful know thee to be a spiritual furnace, O Theo-tok-

os;   for even as the Most Ex-alted One saved the Three

Youths,   so also was the whole world renewed in thy womb by

Him   Who is the praised and most glorious God of our fath-ers.

Ode 8:

In the furnace as in a forge   the Children of Is-rael shone

with the beauty of piety purer than gold, say-ing: Bless

Appendix 6

Appendix 6 139

Appendix 6   141

THE EIRMOSI TONES

THIRD TONE, Ode 1:

He that of old by a Di-vine com-mand gath-ered the waters together into a single as-sem-bly and di-vid-ed the sea for the Israel-ite peo-ple: this is our God Who is glo-ri-fied. To Him alone let us sing, for He is glo-ri-fied.

Ode 3:

O Most High, Rul-er of all, Who brought-est forth all things out of non-be-ing, cre-a-ting them by Thy Word, and per-fect-ing them by Thy Spir-it: Make me stead-fast in Thy love.

Ode 4:

Thou didst show a might-y love for us, O Lord; for Thou

Appendix 6

Appendix 6

Appendix 6

Fifth Tone, Ode 9, continued:

O-rient is His Name.   In mag-ni-fy-ing Him,   we call the

Vir - gin bless - ed.

Appendix 6

Appendix 6   155

The Eirmosi Tones

Sixth Tone, Ode 9, conclusion.

with the heav-enly hosts, we call thee bless - - - - ed.

Appendix 6 157

Appendix 6 159

Appendix 6

Appendix 7:

Melodies for "It is truly meet"

Appendix 7

Appendix 8:

The Typicon on "Disorderly Shrieks" and other commentary

Typicon, Chapter 28

Concerning disorderly shrieks

The disorderly shriek of those who sing in church is not to be accepted as church singing. Whosoever admits it as church singing (i.e., indulges in the admitted shrieks) shall not be ac-cepted: let them be deposed from their rank, and let them not sing again in church. For it is fitting to sing in good order, and to send up glory in concord to the Lord and master of All, as with one mouth, from our heart. Those who disobey this are subject to eternal torment, for they do not submit themselves to the tradition and rules of the Holy Fathers.

Canon 75 of the Sixth Ecumenical Council

We wish those who attend church for the purpose of chanting neither to employ disorderly cries and to force nature to cry out aloud, nor to foist in anything that is not becoming and proper to a church; but, on the contrary, to offer such psalmodies with much attentiveness and contriteness to God, who sees directly into everything that is hidden from our sight. *"For the sons of Israel shall be reverent"* (Lev. 15:30), the sacred word has taught us.

Interpretation. The chanting, or psalmody, that is done in churches is in the nature of begging God to be appeased for our sins. Whoever begs and prayerfully supplicates must have a humble and contrite manner; but to cry out manifests a manner that is audacious and irreverent. On this account the present Canon commands that those who chant in the churches refrain from forcing their nature to yell, but also from saying anything else that is unsuitable for the church. But what are the things that are unsuitable for the church? The expositor Zonaras replies that they are womanish members and warblings (which is the same as saying trills, and an excessive variation or modulation in melodies which inclines towards the songs sung by harlots). The present Canon, therefore, commands that all these things be eliminated from the Church, and those that chant therein shall offer their psalmodies with great care to God, who looks into the hidden recesses of the heart, i.e., into the psalmody and prayer that are framed mentally in the heart rather than uttered in external cries. For the sacred word of Leviticus teaches us sons of Israel to be reverent to God. (212)

(212) That is why divine Chrysostom (Hom. on "I saw the Lord sitting on a throne," p. 120, vol. v) strenuously prohibits theatrical singing, dances of gesticulators, and prolonged cries and yells, and disorderly intonations. For in interpreting that passage in the Psalms saying "Serve the Lord in fear" (Ps. 2:11), he severely censures those who mingle the secular gestures of theaters with spiritual songs, and who admix therewith theatrical postures and meaningless intonations (such as are nowadays the trills and quavers and other meaningless utterances); and he says that these things are natural, not to those engaged in doxologizing God, but to those playing, and mingling the sports of demons with angelic doxology. By means of many arguments he teaches that we ought to offer up doxologies to God with fear and a contrite heart, in order that they may be welcome, like fragrant incense. What Meletius Pegas, a very learned man, says in his third discourse concerning Christianity is in truth to be praised and deserving of all admiration: "Precisely, therefore, as modesty and symmetry of music is attractive, it is adapted to render hearts more robust, by drawing the soul up from the body. For harmony is most agreeable to the spirit, having as it does an intermediate nature partaking of the crassness of the body, combined with the immateriality of the spirit. Thus, again excessive music, pursuing what is sweet beyond moderation fails to excite pleasure, but, on the contrary, tends to enervate . . . for it is on this account that only the human voice finds acceptance in the Church, on the ground that it is inherent in nature and unartificial, whereas the percussions and efflations produced by instruments are sent packing by the divine

Fathers on the ground that they are too artificial." Yet some of the musicians of today are striving to put these things back into the Church with their instru-mental songs. The trills and quavers that are now being chanted do not appear to be old, but, on the contrary, modernistic, in view of the fact in the songs ascribed to John Damascene and other musi-cians of olden times such meaningless words and prolongations; they appear to have come into exist-ence about the time of John Koukouzelos. But the prolongations which the psalts of today are chant-ing in the vigils, being double and often triple the standard length are in truth nauseating and become offensive to reverent listeners. Wherefore we beseech canonical psalts to chant their songs more quickly, in order that their songs may at the same time be more tuneful, and in order to leave time for reading to be done; accordingly, the canons may be chanted more slowly, in which is rooted all the soulful (or psychical) fruit of the vigil. Some say, however, that these meaningless trills were in-troduced into the Church with a view to attracting the simple laity by means of their pleasant effect on the ear.

The 85 canons of apostles (sarasotaorthodox.com)

"Singing and music in general, have a much more profound meaning and significance than is commonly thought. It is a genuine language of nature used by all that lives: man, as well as beasts, birds, and reptiles…

…Prayer, as the supreme expression of man's spirit in this world, often seeks and finds a form for itself in harmonious musical sounds which serve not merely as a beautiful attire for it but also give it wings on which it soars to heaven where glorious singing, that invariable lan-guage of the angels, never ceases.

If the same harmony reigned on earth as reigns in the highest, then hymns of praise to the Creator of the worlds would resound unceasingly here also, and man's tongue would be like music, of the sort we hear sometimes on the lips of simple folk, children, and chaste youth, as well as all those who have a joyful and serene heart.

+Metropolitan Anastassy (Gribanovsky)

(From **Discourse with One's Own Heart**)

УКАЗ КЛИРУ И ЦЕРКОВНЫМ ПЕВЧИМ

Надлежит всегда помнить и сознавать, что церковное пение есть молитва и, что пение молитв должно совершаться благоговейно, для возбуждения к молитве стоящих в церкви. Недопустимы напевы и песнопения лишь услаждающие слух, но по содержанию или исполнению нерасполагающие к молитве, а также несоответствующие данному богослужению, событию, отмечаемому церковью, дню и церковному уставу. Вместе с тем поведение поющих должно быть благоговейным и соответствующим высокому званию церковных певцов, соединяющих голоса свои с голосами ангелов.

Наблюдение за тем лежит на обязанности руководителей пения и на совершающем богослужение священнослужителе, указания коего должны исполняться беспрекословно.

УКАЗ О НЕДОПУСТИМОСТИ УЧАСТИЯ В РАЗВЕСЕЛЕНИЯХ В КАНУН ВОСКРЕСНЫХ И ПРАЗДНИЧНЫХ ДНЕЙ

Священные правила повествуют, чтобы кануны праздничных дней проводились христианами в молитве и благоговении, подготовляясь к участию или присутствию на Божественной литургии. Если к тому призываются все православные христиане, то тем более то касается непосредственно принимающих участие в церковной службе. Участие их в развлечениях в кануны праздников особенно греховно. Ввиду сего, бывшие в канун Воскресения или Праздника на балу или подобных развлечениях и увеселениях не могут на следующий день участвовать в хоре, прислуживать, входить в алтарь и становиться на клирос.

Ukase addressed to clergy and church singers

It is always necessary to remember and be aware that church singing is prayer, and prayers must be chanted with reverence in order to stimulate the faithful who stand in church to pray. Chants and hymns which only delight the ear but by content or manner of performance do not dispose one to prayer are unacceptable. The same applies to those chants and hymns which are incompatible with the given church service, commemoration, or church rubrics. In addition, the behavior of the singers must be reverent and compatible with the high calling of church singers, who unite their voices with the voices of the angels. It is the responsibility of the choir director and the celebrating priest to oversee this, and the priest's directives must be fulfilled without question.

Ukase concerning the inadmissibility of engaging in entertainments on the eves of feast days

The holy canons dictate that Christians should spend the eves of feast days in prayer and with reverence in preparation for participation or attendance at the Divine Liturgy. If all Orthodox Christians are called to this, then this pertains all the more to those who take an active part in the church service itself. Their participation in diversions on the eve of a feast day is especially sinful. In view of the above, those who attend a dance or similar form of entertainment and diversion may not participate in the choir the next day, may not serve in the altar, enter the altar or stand on the cliros.

+ Архиепископъ Іоаннъ

Archbishop John (Maximovich)

Appendix 9:

Vowel formation chart

Приложение 9.

Vowel formation chart

Схема образования гласных звуков

Tongue vowels   Lip vowels

Языковые гласные   Губные гласные

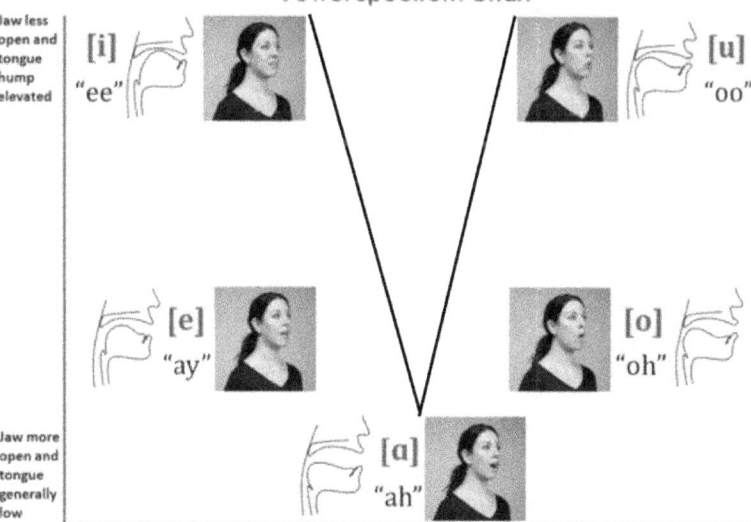

Appendix 10:
On breath control

Приложение 10.

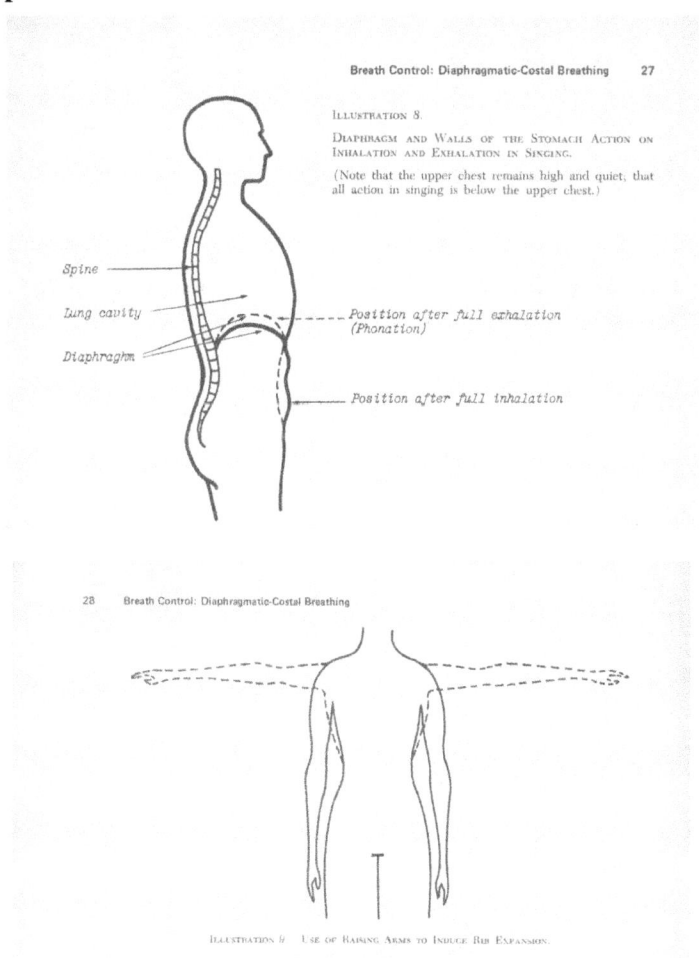

From **Foundations in Singing. 3rd edition. Van A. Christy.**

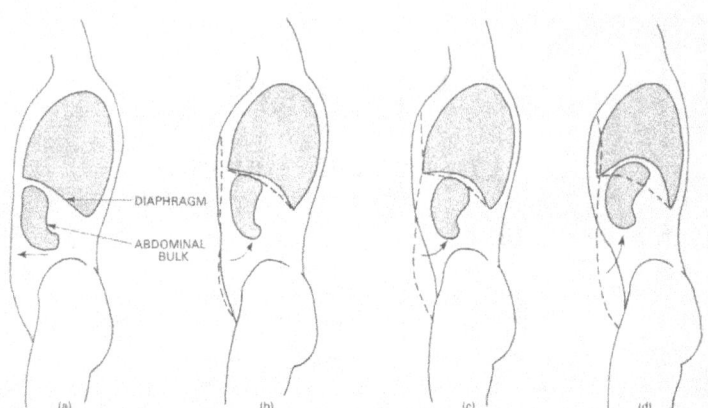

Fig. 3. a. Inhalation. b. Shortly after beginning of phrase. c. Continuation of phrase. d. End of phrase. Dotted lines in b, c, and d represent original positions of chest, belly, and diaphragm.

Singing Technique, How to Avoid Vocal Trouble. Klein, Joseph J. & Schjeide, Ole A. National Music Publishers, 1981. p.18.

Appendix 11:

Some websites with liturgical music

Some Websites with Orthodox Liturgical Music

http://rocm.org/

http://kliros.ru/

http://regentlib.orthodoxy.ru/

https://www.sobor.org/russian-liturgical-music-archive

http://www.voinov.org/cgi-bin/music/Scores

https://horist.ru/

http://orthodoxia.org/music/

http://agiosis.orthodoxy.ru/arhiv.htm

https://music.russianorthodox-stl.org/ (English)

https://www.regentzagod.com/notes

https://www.orthodoxchoral.org/ (Russian and English)

http://www.oca.org/liturgics/music-downloads Music Downloads - Orthodox Church in America (oca.org)

Православная церковная музыка и пение - Православное христианство (www.hristianstvo.ru/culture/music/churchmusic/)

notymus.narod.ru)

www.orthodoxrussiansinging.com)

Библиотека Московской регентско-певческой семинарии (seminaria.ru)

Appendix 12:

On bell ringing: Fr. Seraphim Slobodskoy and N. V. Matveev

ABOUT THE BELLS AND THE RUSSIAN ORTHODOX RINGING[8]

Archpriest Seraphim Slobodskoy

Bells are one of the most essential elements of an Orthodox Church. In the "Order of the Blessing of Bells" we read, "So let all that hear them ring, either during the day or at night, be inspired to the glorification of Thy saints". Church-bell ringing is used to:

- Summon the faithful to the divine services.
- Express the triumphal joy of the Church and Her divine services.
- Announce to those not present in the church the times of especially important moments in the services.

In addition, in some cites in Old Russia, bells summoned the people to gatherings. Also, bells were used to guide those lost in bad weather, and announced various dangers or misfortunes such as fires or floods. In days of peril to the nation they called the people to her defense. Bells proclaimed military victories and greeted those returning from the field of battle. Thus bells played a great part in the life of the Russian people. Bells were usually hung in special belltowers constructed over the Entry to a church or beside it.

Bells did not come into use immediately after the appearance of Christianity. In the Old Testament Church, in the Temple in Jerusalem, the

---

[8] Slobodskoy, Prot. Seraphim. Law of God. 1973. Ed. 3. Printing house of Job Pochaevsky. Jordanville, N.J. Art. 699–711.

faithful were summoned to services not with bells, but with trumpets. In the first centuries of Christianity, when the Church was persecuted by the pagans, Christians had no opportunity to openly call the faithful to services. At that time, they were secretly summoned either by one of the deacons or special messengers, or sometimes the bishop himself at the end of a service would reveal the time and place of the next one.

Following the cessation of persecutions in the fourth century, various means came into use to summon the faithful. More specific means were found in the sixth century when the sound of boards or iron hoops, beaten with hammers, summoned the faithful. Eventually the most perfect means of calling the faithful to the services was devised, pealing bells.

The first bells, as is well known, appeared in Western Europe. There is a tradition by which the invention of bells is ascribed to St. Paulinus the Bishop of Nola (411) at the end of the fourth or the beginning of the fifth century. Several versions of this tradition exist. In one, St. Paulinus saw some field flowers in a dream, daffodils, which gave forth a pleasant sound. When he awoke the bishop ordered bells cast, which had the form of these flowers. But, evidently, St. Paulinus did not introduce bells into the practice of the Church, since neither in his works nor in the works of his contemporaries are bells mentioned. Only in the beginning of the seventh century did the Pope of Rome, Sabinian, successor to St. Gregory the Dialogist, succeed in giving bells a Christian significance. From this period, bells began gradually to be used by Christians, and in the course of the eighth and ninth centuries in Western Europe, bells properly became part of Christian liturgical practice.

In the East, in the Greek Church, bells came into use in the second half of the ninth century, when in 865, the Doge of Venice, Ursus, gave the Emperor Michael a gift of twelve large bells. These bells were hung in a tower near Hagia Sophia Cathedral. But bells did not come into general use among the Byzantines.

In Russia, bells appeared almost simultaneously with the reception of Christianity by St. Vladimir (988 A.D.). Wooden boards and metal hoops beaten with hammers were also used and still are in some monasteries. But strangely enough, Russia took bells not from Greece from whence she received Orthodoxy, but from Western Europe. The very word kolokol comes from the German word "glocke". The Slavonic word is kampan which comes from the Roman province of Campania where the first bells, made of bronze, were cast. Initially the bells were small, and each church had only two or three.

In the fifteenth century special factories for bell casting appeared, where bells of huge proportions were made. In the bell tower of Ivan the Great in Moscow, for example, are the "Everyday" bell weighing 36,626 pounds; the bell "reyute" weighing 72,000 pounds; and the largest bell, called "Dormition", which weighs around 144,000 pounds.

The largest bell in the world at present is the "Tsar Bell". It stands on a stone pedestal at the base of the bell tower of Ivan the Great. There is no equal to it in the world, not only in dimension and weight, but in the fine art of casting. The "Tsar Bell" was poured by Russian masters Ivan and Mikail Matorin, father and son, in 1733–1735. Material for the "Tsar Bell" was taken from its predecessor, a gigantic bell which had been damaged in a fire. This bell weighed 288,000 pounds and was cast by the master craftsman, Alexander Grigoriev, in 1654. To the 288,000 pounds of base metal was added more than 80,000 pounds of alloy. In all, the total weight of the Tsar Bell is 218 American tons. The diameter of the bell is 6 meters, 60 centimeters, or 21 feet, 8 inches.

This amazing product of casting was never successfully hung for it was severely damaged in a terrible and devastating fire in 1737. Still in its casting form on a wooden scaffolding, it is not known whether or not it was ever hung from this scaffolding. When the wooden scaffolding caught fire, they started to throw water on it. The red hot bell developed many large and small cracks due to the extreme change in temperature, and a large piece, weighing 11,000 kilograms (11.5 tons), fell from the bell.

After the fire, the "Tsar Bell" lay in its casting form for a whole century. In 1836, the bell was lifted out and placed on a stone pedestal, the project of the architect A. Montferrand, the builder of St. Isaac's Cathedral and the Alexander Column in Petersburg. It stands on this pedestal now with the fallen piece of the bell leaning at the foot of the pedestal. Such is the fate of the largest bell in the world, the "Tsar Bell", which was never rung.

The largest working bell is the "Dormition" bell, located in Moscow, at the bell tower of Ivan the Great. Its pealing gave the signal to begin the festive ringing of the bells of all the Moscow churches on Pascha night. Thus, the Russian Orthodox people loved the ringing of the church bells and enriched the craft with their innovation and art.

The distinguishing quality of Russian bells is their sonority and melodiousness. This is attained by various techniques:
- An exact proportion of bronze and tin, often with silver added, the proper alloy.
- The height of the bell and its width, the right proportions.
- The thickness of the walls of the bell.
- The correct hanging of the bell.
- The correct composition of the tongue and its manner of being hung in the bell.

Russians call the clapper, the tongue. The Russian bell is distinguished from the Western European bell in that it is fixed in position, and the clapper moves and strikes the sides of the bell, which produces the sound. It is characteristic that the Russian people call the movable part of the bell the "tongue", enabling the bell to have a living voice and trumpet. Truly, with what other name, if not a talking one, can one call the bell?

On the days of great feasts the sound of the bell reminds us of the blessedness of Heaven. On the days of great saints, it reminds us of the eternal repose of the dwellers of Heaven. During the days of Holy Week, it reminds us of our reconciliation with God through Christ the Savior. On the days of Bright Week, it proclaims the victory of life over death and the eternal, endless joy of the future life in the Kingdom of Christ.

Is it not a mouth that speaks when the bell tells us of each passing hour, and reminds us of the passage of time and of eternity when there should be time no longer (Rev. 10:6).

Announcing the glory of the name of Christ, day and night, from the heights of a church of God, the sound of bells reminds us of the words of the Lord, the Pantocrator, spoken through the Old Testament Prophet Isaiah, *I have set watchmen upon thy walls, O Jerusalem, which shall never hold their peace day nor night* (Is. 62:6). It is not by chance that pagans, when they heard the sound of bells, often said, "that is the voice of the Christian God".

The sound of one church bell is something exalted and solemn, and if there are several bells in harmony with each other, then a more magnificent sonority is sounded. A moving peal of bells acts upon our inner feelings and awakens our souls from spiritual slumber. What grieved, despondent, and often irritating tones are evoked by church bells in the soul of an evil and impious apostate. The feelings of discomfort and weariness of soul are evoked by the sound of the bell in the soul of a perpetual sinner. But in the soul of the faithful, who seek peace with God the Lord, the church bell awakens a bright, joyous, and serene disposition. Thus a person can define the state of his soul by means of the sound of bells.

One can bring forth examples from life, when a man, exhausted from fighting life's bitterness, and fallen into despair and despondency, decides to take his own life. Then he hears the church bell. Preparing to commit suicide, he trembles, becomes afraid, and involuntarily guards himself with the sign of the Cross. It recalls the Heavenly Father, and new, good feelings arise in his soul, and the one who was perishing forever returns to life. Thus, in the strokes of a church bell there is hidden a wonderful power, which penetrates deeply into the soul of mankind.

Having loved the sound of the church bell, Orthodox people associate it with all their festive and sorrowful events. Therefore, the sound of the Orthodox belltower serves not only to indicate the time of divine services, but also to express joy, grief and festivity. Various forms of bell ringing, each with their own name and meaning, developed to express this range of feelings.

The Forms of Bell Ringing and Their Names

The manner of church bell ringing is divided into two basic forms: 1. the measured ringing of the bell to announce church services, and 2. ringing of all the bells.

Ringing to Announce Church Services.

By the "announcement of church services" is meant the measured strokes of one large bell. By this sound, the faithful are called together to the temple of God for divine services. In Russian it is known as the "Good news bell" because it announces the blessed, good news of the beginning of divine services.

The "good news peal" is accomplished thus. First there are produced three widely spaced, slow, prolonged strokes, so as to sustain the sound of the bell, followed by measured strokes. If the bell is very heavy or of great dimensions, the measured strokes are produced by the swinging of the clapper from side to side of the bell. If the bell is of medium size, then its clapper is drawn sufficiently close to the rim by a rope. The rope is attached to a wooden foot pedal, and with pressure from the bell-ringer's feet, the sound is produced.

The "good news peal" is subdivided in turn into two types:

1) The usual or hourly peal, produced with the largest bell.

2) The lenten or occasional peal, produced on the next largest bell on weekdays of the Great Fast.

If the church has several large bells, as is usually the case in cathedrals or large monasteries, then the size of the bells corresponds to their significance: 1) the holiday bell, 2) the Sunday bell, 3) the polyeleos bell, 4) the daily bell, and 5) the fifth, or small bell. Usually in parishes there are no more that two or three large bells.

The ringing of all the bells is subdivided as follows:

1) Trezvon (Peal) — thrice-sounded, multiple bell ringing. This is the simultaneous ringing of all the bells, then a brief pause, a second ringing of all the bells, again a brief pause, and a third ringing of all the bells, i.e., a simultaneous ringing of all the bells three times, or a ringing in three refrains.

2) Dvuzvon — twice rung. This is the simultaneous ringing of all the bells twice, in two refrains.

3) Perezvon (Chain Ringing) — this is the ringing of each bell in turn, with either one or several strokes of each bell, beginning with the largest to the very smallest, and then repeating several times.

4) Perebor (Toll) — This is the slow, single peal of each bell in turn, beginning with the smallest to the largest, and after the stroke on the largest bell all the bells are immediately struck together; then this is repeated several times.

The Use of the Bells and its Meaning

Bells For All-night Vigil

1) Before the beginning of the All-night Vigil — the "good news peal", which concludes with the simultaneous ringing of all the bells, or the trezvon.

2) At the beginning of the reading of the Six Psalms comes the twice-rung, simultaneous peal, the dvuzvon. The dvuzvon announces the beginning of the second part of the All-night Vigil — Matins. It expresses the joy of the Resurrection of Christ, the incarnation of the Second person of the Holy Trinity, our Lord, Jesus Christ. The beginning of Matins, as we know, recalls the Birth of Christ, and begins with the doxology of the angels in their revelation to the shepherds of Bethlehem, Glory to God in the highest, and on earth peace, good will among men.

In popular usage, the twice-rung bell at the All-night Vigil is called the second-bell (the second bell peal after the beginning of the All-night Vigil).

3) At the time of the singing of the polyeleos, before the reading of the Gospel, the trezvon, the thrice performed, simultaneous ringing of all the bells, is rung, expressing joy in celebrating the event.

At the Sunday All-night Vigil, this ringing expresses the joy and festivity of the Resurrection of Christ. In some localities it is performed at the time of the chanting, "In that we have beheld the Resurrection of Christ..." Customarily in guide books, this peal is called the "bells before the Gospel".

In popular usage, the trezvon in the All-night Vigil (the bells before the Gospel) is called the "third ringing".

4) At the beginning of the Song of the Most-holy Theotokos, "My soul doth magnify the Lord...", occurs a short good news peal, composed of nine strokes of the large bell (customary in Kiev and in all of Little Russia).

5) On Great Feasts, at the conclusion of the Vigil, the trezvon occurs.

6) At Pontifical services, after every All-night Vigil, the trezvon is rung, accompanying the bishop as he leaves the church.

The Bells for the Liturgy

Before the beginning of the reading of the Third Hour, the good news peal for the Liturgy is rung, and at the end of the Sixth Hour, before the beginning of the Liturgy, the trezvon.

If two Liturgies are served (an early one and a later one), then the good news peal for the early Liturgy is simpler and slower than the one for the later Liturgy, and it is customarily done not using the large bell.

At Pontifical divine services, the good news peal for the Liturgy begins at the indicated time. As the bishop approaches the church, the trezvon is rung. When the bishop enters the church, the trezvon ceases and the good news peal resumes and continues throughout the vesting of the bishop. At the end of the Sixth Hour, the trezvon is rung again. Then, during the Liturgy, the good news peal is rung at the beginning of the Eucharistic Canon, the most important part of the Liturgy, to announce the time of the sanctification and the transformation of the Holy Gifts.

According to T.K. Nikolsky, in the book *Ustav Bogosluzhenia*, it is said that the good news peal before "It is Meet...", begins with the words, "It is meet and right to worship the Father, and the Son, and the Holy Spirit...", and continues until the chanting of "It is truly meet to bless Thee, the Theotokos..." It is also the instruction in the book *Novaia Skrizhal* by Archbishop Benjamin (published in S.P.B., 1908, p. 213). In practice, the good news peal for "It is meet..." is shorter, composed of twelve strokes. In southern Russia the good news peal for "It is meet..." is performed customarily before the beginning of the Eucharistic Canon, at the time of the chanting of the Creed (12 strokes, 1 stroke for each clause of the Creed). The good news peal before "It is meet...", according to the custom of Russian churches was introduced during the time of Patriarch Joachim of Moscow (1690 A.D.), similar to the custom of the West, where they ring during the words "Take, eat...".

At the conclusion of the Liturgy on all Great Feasts the trezvon is rung. Also, after every Liturgy served by a bishop the trezvon is rung to accompany the bishop as he leaves the church.

On the feast of the Nativity, the trezvon is rung all the day of the feast, from Liturgy until Vespers. Also, on the feast of the Resurrection of Christ — Pascha.

The good news peal before Bright Matins begins before the All-night Vigil and continues until the Procession of the Cross, and the festive trezvon is rung from the beginning of the Procession of the Cross to its end and even longer.

Before the Paschal Liturgy, the good news peal and the trezvon are rung. During the Paschal Liturgy itself, at the time of the Gospel reading, the perezvon is rung, with seven strokes on each bell (the number seven expresses the fullness of the glory of God). This festive ringing of bells signals the homily on the Gospel of Christ in all languages. Upon completion of the reading of the Gospel, the perezvon concludes with the joyful, victorious trezvon.

During all of Bright Week, the trezvon occurs every day, from the end of the Liturgy until Vespers. On all Sundays from Pascha until Ascension, after the Liturgy the trezvon is rung.

On the feast day of a church, at the conclusion of the Liturgy before the beginning of the Moleben, the short good news peal and the trezvon are rung, and at the conclusion of the Moleben, the trezvon.

Whenever there is a procession around the church, the trezvon is rung.

Before the Royal Hours, the good news peal is usually rung on the large bell, and before the Great Holy Week Hours, the Lenten good news peal in rung on the small bell. As at the Royal Hours, so also at the Great Holy Week Hours before each Hour the bell is rung. Before the Third Hour the bell is struck three times, before the Sixth Hour, six times and before the Ninth Hour, nine times. Before the Typica and Great Compline, twelve times. If during the fast a feast day is celebrated, then for the Hours they do not strike separately for each Hour.

On Matins of Good Friday, when the Twelve Gospel Readings of the Lord's Passion are read, besides the usual good news peal and trezvon at the beginning of matins, there is a good news peal before each Gospel reading: before the first Gospel reading — one stroke on the large bell, before the second gospel reading — two strokes, before the third Gospel reading — three strokes, etc.

Upon conclusion of Matins, as the faithful carry the "Holy Thursday fire" to their homes, the trezvon is rung.

Use of the Perezvon and its Meaning

At Vespers on Great Friday, before the elevation of the Burial Shroud, at the time of the singing of the last sticheron of the aposticha, a slow perezvon, one stroke on each bell, from the largest to the the smallest, is performed. Upon the placement of the Shroud in the center of the church, the trezvon is rung.

At Matins for Great Saturday, beginning with the chanting of the "Great Doxology" and continuing through the procession with the Shroud around the church, the perezvon is rung the same for the carrying back of the Shroud, a slow perezvon, one stroke on each bell from the largest to the smallest. When they pick up the Shroud in the middle of the church and go with it to the Royal Gates, then the trezvon is rung.

The slow perezvon with one stroke on each bell, beginning with the largest, most powerful sound, and ascending by degrees to the most delicate and highest pitched tone of the small bell, symbolizes the "outpouring (in terms of humility)" of our Lord Jesus Christ for our salvation, as we sing, for example, in the fourth irmos of the Fifth Tone: "Foreseeing Thy divine self-emptying upon the Cross…".

As established by centuries of practice by the Russian Orthodox Church, in the central part of Russia such a perezvon could be performed only twice a year, on Good Friday and Great Saturday, the day of the Crucifixion of the Lord and His burial. Experienced bell-ringers usually follow this custom strictly and do not permit otherwise, so that the sorrowful sound pertaining to the Lord, our Saviour, would be reserved and distinct from the funeral bells of simple, mortal and sinful people.

At Matins on the day of the Elevation of the Cross of the Lord, during the week of the Veneration of the Cross, and on the first of August, before carrying Cross out of the Altar at the time of the chanting of the "Great Doxology", the perezvon occurs, during which they slowly strike three times (in some places, one time) on each bell from the largest to the smallest. When the Cross is carried to the middle of the church and placed on the analogion, the trezvon is rung.

Similarly to the perezvon, but faster and in quick succession, seven or three times on each bell, the bell is rung before the little blessing of water. At the time of the immersion of the Cross in the water, the trezvon is rung.

As before the blessing of water, the perezvon occurs before the ordination of a bishop. In general, the perezvon is quick, but sometimes on each bell there is a festive peal. In several places, such a perezvon is performed before the beginning of the Liturgy on the feast day of the church, or in other instances, for example, as we indicated above, during the reading of the Paschal Gospel.

The Use of the Perebor and its Meaning

The perebor, otherwise known as the funeral bell, expresses grief over the dead. It is used, as we explained above, in the reverse order of the perezvon. That is, slowly they stroke one time on each bell from the smallest to the largest, and after that they strike all the bells simultaneously. This mournful, funeral perebor must conclude with a short trezvon, expressing the joyous Christian faith in the resurrection of the dead.

In view of the fact that in several guides on bell ringing, one is instructed not to play a trezvon at the funeral service of the dead, and as this directive does not correspond to church practice, we will take this opportunity to give some explanation.

The slow perebor ring of the bells, from the smallest to the largest, symbolizes a man's growing up on earth, from small stature to maturity and strength, and the single, simultaneous strike on all the bells signifies that the earthly life of man is stopped by death, because of which all that is acquired by man in this life is left behind. As this is expressed in the hymns of the funeral service, "All mortal things are vanity and exist not after death. Riches endure not, neither does glory accompany on the way; for when death comes, all these things vanish utterly" (or as in another hymn, "yet one moment only, and death shall supplant them all"). Therefore, to the immortal Christ we cry, "Give rest to the one who has passed away, in the abode of those who rejoice". The second part of the hymn directly speaks of the joy of the future life with Christ. This joy is also expressed with the trezvon after the sorrowful perebor.

In the journal *Pravoslavnaia Rus'* (*Orthodox Russia*), Archbishop Averky, according to the custom of the occasion at funerals and Pannykhidas for the deceased, gave the soundly based explanation which, without doubt pertains to the bells as well. 'According to our Orthodox custom, to perform Pannykhidas and funerals, bright clothing is put on. The custom of celebrating these orders of worship in black clothing came to us from the West, and is absolutely uncharacteristic of the spirit of Orthodoxy. Nevertheless, it is widespread among us. So much so, that now it is not easy to eradicate. For true Christians, death is a passage to better life, joy and not sorrow, as is beautifully expressed in the moving third kneeling prayer read at Vespers on the day of Pentecost, 'Because there is no death, O Lord, for Thy servants when we depart from the body and come to Thee, our God, but a change from things very sorrowful unto things most beneficial and most sweet, and unto repose and gladness."

The trezvon, reminiscent of the Resurrection, gracefully acts in the soul of the Christian believer, grieving over the separation from the deceased, and gives it internal consolation. To deprive the Christian of such comfort has no basis, the more so since this trezvon has fundamentally entered into the life of the Russian Orthodox people and has become an expression of their faith. In this way, as the body of the deceased is brought to the funeral in the church, there is the mournful perebor, and as it is being carried into the church, the trezvon. After the funeral, upon carrying the deceased out of the church, there again occurs the perebor, concluding also with the trezvon.

During the funerals and burials of priests, hieromonks, archimandrites and bishops, a slightly different perebor is performed. First they strike the large bell twelve times, then follows the perebor; again the twelve strokes on the large bell, and again the perebor, etc. As the body is brought into the church, the trezvon is rung; also during the reading of the prayer of absolution — the trezvon. During the removal of the body, again the perebor is indicated, and upon the placing of the body in the grave, the trezvon occurs. In other places, the bells are rung according to the usual custom for funerals.

In the *Chinovnei Knige*, it is said that during the removal of Patriarch Joachim, there was a good news peal, alternately on all the bells (Vrem. Mask. Obshch. 1st. i drevi. 1852, vol. 15, p.22).

Not long ago we had occasion to learn that there exists still one other form of perebor. It is one stroke on each bell, but beginning with the largest to the smallest, and then a simultaneous striking of all the bells. This was put on a record, Rostovskie Zvoni (Rostov Bells), recorded in Rostov on 1963. In practice we have not heard such ringing, and there are no directions about them. Therefore we are unable to indicate where and when this pattern is used.

There also exists the so-called "beautiful ringing" on all the bells. The "beautiful ringing" exists at cathedral gatherings, monasteries, wherever they have a large collection of bells. The "beautiful ringing" is composed of several bellringers in a company of five or more people. The beautiful ringing occurs on the great feast days, at festive and joyful events of the Church, and also for greeting the bishop of the diocese.

It is also necessary to mention the "alarm bell", which serves a social purpose. By "alarm bell" is meant the uninterrupted, frequent strokes on the large bell. The "alarm bell" is used to alert people in the case of fire, flood, mutiny, invasion by an enemy, or some other form of social calamity.

The "vetchevnie" bell was used to call all the inhabitants of ancient Novgorod and Pskov to the vetche, or popular assembly.

Victories over the enemy and regiments returning from the fields of battle were announced with the joyous, festive trezvon on all the bells.

In conclusion, we note that Russian bellringers attained high mastery of bell ringing and were famous throughout the world. Many tourists came from Europe, England and America to the feast of Pascha in Moscow, to hear the Paschal bells.

On the "Feast of Feasts" in Moscow, the bells of all its churches, numbering more than 5,000, were rung. Thus, whoever heard the Paschal bells of Moscow would never forget it. It was "a unique symphony," as writer I. Shmelov expressed it. This powerful, festive sound permeated to Heaven a victorious hymn to the Resurrection of Christ.

(The basic description of the order of bell ringing is laid down for the most part in Practice of the Russian Church in Central Russia. The description of practice was compiled and confirmed by the many events and daily practices of the Russian Orthodox people, by the very life of the Orthodox Church).

Bell chimes[9]

N.V. Matveev

A typical Russian phenomenon was the art of bell ringing, which reached a high development in Russia. Bells have been used in Russian churches since the middle of the 11th century, replacing the so-called "bila" – cast-iron strips that were hit with a hammer to announce the beginning of a church service. Bell ringing in Russia was brought to the level of a high and subtle art. Sets of bells of different sizes, structures, strengths and colors of sound made it possible to produce bright and effective "music". Along with their own chants, various church parishes and monasteries developed also their own styles of bell ringing.

Bells are a necessary accessory of Orthodox churches and are placed either on the roof of the church, in the towers of the domes, or at the entrances to the church, in belfries arranged in the arches of the porch and in the church itself on the western side, or near the church in a special building for them, called the bell tower.

Church bells are designed to:

1) announce the service, call the people to the service;

2) to express the triumph of the Church and her services; and

3) to announce to those who are not present in the temple about the well-known prayers and readings of the divine services performed in the temple, and, thus, to call on them to join their prayers to the Lord with the prayers of those in the church.

In addition, the bells had another use – in rural churches they served for travelers (during blizzards and snowstorms) as a saving guide.

---

[9] Choral singing. N.V. Matveev. 1998. Ed. Brotherhood of St. good. Prince Alexander Nevsky. Art.265-274.

Bells in the church Typicon are called by the words: *bilo, klepalo, kampan, tyazhkaya, zvony*.

Some of these names have survived from the time when bells were not yet used in the Christian church (before the 8th century) and the faithful were called to worship by means of a wooden or metal board, which was hit with a hammer or stick. This board or stick in the Typicon is called *bilo, klepalo, drevo*. When the boards were replaced by bells, what was said in the Typicon about the *bilo, klepalo, drevo* came to be applied to the bells. Bells themselves in the Typicon are indicated by the words:

kampan – from the name of the Roman province of Campania, where copper was mined, from which the first bells were cast;

tyazhkaya (heavy) – from the heavy, strong sounds of bells;

zvony (rings) – from the sonority of bells.

Usually in churches there are several bells, different in size and sound strength:

1) festive,

2) Sunday,

3) polyeleos,

4) everyday,

5) a fifth, or small bell.

In addition, there are several small ringing bells of various sizes.

The ringing of bells before the start of the service, during it and after the service is not the same. There are mainly two types of ringing: the **blagovest** and the **zvon**.

Blagovest is a type of ringing when one bell is struck. If several bells are strung, not together, but each bell alternately, then the blagovest is called *perezvon* or *perebor*.

A **zvon** is a type of ringing when the bells are struck together. When the ringing of several bells occurs in three stages, then it is called a *trezvon*.

The *blagovest* is used to before worship in church: one bell is struck for some time before the start of the service. The bell calling to church, to the service of God, always proclaims joyful, good news, which is why it is called the *blagovest* (good news). Before more solemn services on

Sundays and feasts, the *blagovest* is followed by the ringing of several bells.

Ringing announcing well-known prayers and readings performed in church during the divine service occurs during Matins and the Liturgy.

Before the All-Night Vigil, a *blagovest* is made, then a *trezvon*. Before the beginning of Matins (when the reading of the Six Psalms begins) – a *trezvon*. Then there is a ringing before the Gospel, which begins during the singing of the anabathmoi before the reading of the Matins Gospel.

At Matins during the singing of the Great Doxology (before the removal of the Cross from the altar) on the feast of the Exaltation of the Holy Cross, on the Week of the Adoration of the Cross and on the day of the feast of the Procession of the Holy Cross (August 1), there is a *perezvon*: each bell is struck in turn once, then all of the bells are struck together, and this is repeated two or three times. During the singing "Holy God", when the Cross is transferred to the middle of the church, all of the bells are rung in a *trezvon*.

The same *perezvon* is supposed to be performed on Holy Friday at Vespers before the bringing out of the Shroud, during the singing of "Joseph and Nicodemus took Thee down from the tree" and at Matins on Great Saturday during the singing of the Great Doxology, before carrying the Shroud around the church.

Before the Liturgy, a *blagovest* is done, and then a *trezvon*. During the Liturgy, there is a ringing of one bell at "It is meet and right", i.e. during the most important part of the Liturgy, the Anaphora; the ringing starts from the words "It is meet and right to worship the Father..." – and continues up to the singing of "It is truly meet to bless thee". At the end of the Liturgy on Sundays and feasts, a *trezvon* is made.

There is also a special ringing during the Liturgy on the day of Holy Pascha, during the reading of the Paschal Gospel, when reading each verse of the Gospel, the largest bell is struck once, and at the last verse all of the bells are struck.

On the days of patronal feasts, there is a *blagovest* before the Moleben and a *trezvon* at its beginning and end. During the procession, both at the beginning and during the procession itself, there is also a *trezvon*.

On the days of patronal feasts, before the consecration of water, there is a *perezvon*, starting with the largest and ending with the smallest bell, several times. When the Cross is immersed in water, during the consecration of water, a *trezvon* is made.

The same ringing that occurs before the consecration of water also occurs before the ordination of a bishop.

During the burial of priests, hieromonks, archimandrites and bishops, when their bodies are taken out of the house and when they are carried to the burial site, the chime is the same as when the Cross is taken out on the Feast of the Exaltation, i.e. each of the bells is struck once (and such a *perebor* is repeated two or three times), and the all of the bells are struck together once.

After reading the prayer of absolution and lowering the coffin into the grave, there is a *trezvon*.

On different categories of feasts, different bells are used for the *blagovest* and the *trezvon*, namely:

1) the *festive* bell is used on all twelve great feasts, on patronal feasts, before the Vigil, before the Liturgy, and before Great Vespers;

2) the *Sunday* bell is used on all Sundays and feasts with an All-Night Vigil, as indicated by the Typicon;

3) the *polyeleos* bell is used on feast days with a polyeleos;

4) the *everyday* bell is used on all weekdays;

5) the *fifth*, or *small* bell is used for the *blagovest* before Little Vespers.

The ringing of bells during Great Lent differs in character from the ringing at other times and is slower. In contrast to this, any other ringing is called "beautiful" by the Typicon.

The Typicon sets the amount of time for the *blagovest* and for ringing before services. The *blagovest* before the All-Night Vigil, as indicated in the Typicon, should last the amount of time during which the Psalm 50 is read once.

On great feasts (Pascha, Annunciation, etc.), a longer *blagovest* is assigned. According to the ruling of the Holy Synod in 1722, it is appropriate "to call for Vespers, Matins and Liturgies without any excesses".

Bell ringing was known in Russia already in the 10th century. Bells in Russia are mentioned in the Chronicle in 988. Bells came not from Byzantium, but from the West. The word *kolokol* (bell), according to some researchers, comes from the old Russian *kolo* – a circle. Others believe that it was composed as follows: *kol o kol* , i.e. the impact of one stake on another, which resembles the ancient *bilo*. There is also a third opinion of some scholars that the word *kolokol* comes from the Greek *kalkun*, meaning a beater or rivet.

At the beginning of the 11th century bells were installed at the churches of St. Sophia in Novgorod, the Church of the Tithes in Kyiv, as well as in some Russian cities – Vladimir, Polotsk, Novgorod-Seversky. The Russians themselves began to cast bells for the first time in the middle of the 13th century in Kyiv.

In the 14th century we find masters in Moscow casting bells for the churches of Moscow and Novgorod. In the 16th century, foundry art flourished in Moscow. Many bells were cast not only for Moscow, but also for other cities. Of the Russian masters of this time, the famous Andrey Chokhov is known. He cast the huge cannon, known as the *Tsar Cannon* (1586), on which Tsar Fyodor Ivanovich is skillfully depicted.

The manufacture of bells, borrowed by us from Germany, developed in Russia in the 17th century, reaching such proportions that were not known in Western Europe. The reason for this lies in the religiosity of the Russian people. The mighty and harmonious ringing of church bells, which had a calming effect on the soul, immediately struck a chord in their heart; in this *blagovest* one hears the great call of Heaven, calling us away from earthly vanity and anxiety. In the 16th century in Moscow, there were at least five thousand bells in all of the churches, which is an average of more than 12 bells for each church.

The size and weight of Russian bells significantly exceeds the size of bells in Western Europe.

In 1735, in the Moscow Kremlin, the Russian bell maker Mikhail Motorin cast the world's largest bell, weighing 12,000 *puds*, i.e. about 200 tons, known as the *Tsar Bell*. The bell remained until 1737 in an earthen pit, in which the entire casting process took place. A wooden shed was built over the pit to cover the bell. In the spring of that year, a great fire broke out in Moscow, which also engulfed the Kremlin buildings. A wooden building over the pit caught fire, where burning logs began to fall. The bell became hot from the heat. From the artistic side, the bell, the sound of which has never been heard, is remarkable for the beauty of its shape and decorations.

After the Tsar Bell, the next largest was the bell of the Holy Trinity-St. Sergius Laura, weighing more than 4000 *puds*, i.e. more than 64 tons, cast in 1748. Next was the Great Dormition Bell in the Moscow Kremlin, weighing also 4000 *puds*, which was cast in 1817 to replace the bell destroyed in 1812 during the explosion that took place during the retreat of Napoleon from Moscow; it had been cast in 1760 and weighed 3,351 *puds* (53.5 tons). Bells up to 1000 *puds* (16 tons) were located in many monasteries.

The ringing on the Ivan the Great bell tower in the Moscow Kremlin was unusually solemn, especially when all of bells were used on the biggest feasts and on solemn occasions; it was called "the beautiful peal" and had its own special melody.

On the night before the Bright Resurrection of Christ, the beautiful peal was made in a special way, according to a long-established Muscovite custom. The ringing for Matins began from the bell tower of Ivan the Great in the Kremlin. For greater splendor and solemnity of the moment, all Moscow churches had to wait until the huge Dormition bell on that bell tower was struck. At its first blow, in the distance, like an echo, the bell of the Strastnoy Monastery echoed, and then the bells of all Moscow churches immediately began to ring. Solemnity spread, expanding, like a wide sound wave, rolling from the Kremlin hill over the Moscow River and spreading far around.

Of all Russian bells, the famous Rostov bells stand out, which are known throughout Russia and are mentioned in many historical monuments.

On the bell tower of the Rostov Cathedral of the Dormition, the bells were tuned to specific pitches. There were thirteen bells in all.

The first, largest bell, the *Sysoi*, weighed 2,000 *puds* (32 tons), and was cast in Rostov in 1689. The tone of this bell corresponded to the sound *do* of the large octave. In addition to the main tone *do*, this bell also gave an upper harmonic tone, which is a decima of the corresponding note *mi* of the small octave.

The second bell, *Polyeleiny*, weighing 1,000 *puds* (16 tons), was cast in 1683 in Rostov. The tone of this bell corresponded to the sound *mi* of the large octave and so is a major third above the main tone *do* emitted by the first large bell.

The third bell, *the Swan*, at 500 puds (8 tons), was cast in 1682. The tone of this bell was tuned to *sol* of the large octave and so was a perfect fifth above the *do* emitted by the first large bell. The tones of these three large bells thus made up a pleasant C major chord.

The rest of the bells had different weights and different tones, but all were in the C major scale of natural and harmonic major. Such a tuning allowed a great variety and euphony of ringing.

On Sundays and feasts, all bells were rung by five bell ringers. This complete ringing is threefold:

1) the *Ioninsky*, named after Metropolitan Jonah, who ruled the Rostov Diocese from 1652 to 1691;

2) the *Akimovsky,* named after Archbishop Joachim, who ruled the Rostov diocese from 1731 to 1741;

3) the *Egoryevsky,* named after Bishop George, who ruled the Rostov diocese from 1718 to 1731.

On weekdays the ringing was done by one ringer using 6 bells. All chimes are based on C major chords. Rostov chimes are the pinnacle of the Russian art of bell ringing.

The Russian people in ancient times paid attention to the harmonious combination of bell ringing. Each chime had its own purpose – a sad death peal, or a cheerful ringing – the beautiful peal, when joy, a great feast, victory, or deliverance from danger were announced.

In ancient Russia, ringing replaced music, because other than the harp, there were almost no musical instruments.

Many monasteries, and especially the Trinity-Sergius Laura, were famous for their melodic ringing, where the art of ringing was passed on successively, from one ringer to another.

Church bells, the Russian people say, involuntarily tear all thoughts from the earth and carry them to the heavenly heights and fill the heart with a joyful, bright feeling. Even now, upon hearing the *blagovest*, a believer makes the sign of the cross and remembers God.

This is the great moral significance of church bells, because they remind us of eternal truth, of great Christian love, and of the existence of God.

Church bell ringing in Russia over several centuries has developed into a certain system of musical sound, representing a special form of Russian national musical art.

Appendix 12

Г. Егорьевский звон.

Д. Будничный звон.

Е. Будничный звон, употребляемый от Недели Фоминой до отдания Пасхи.

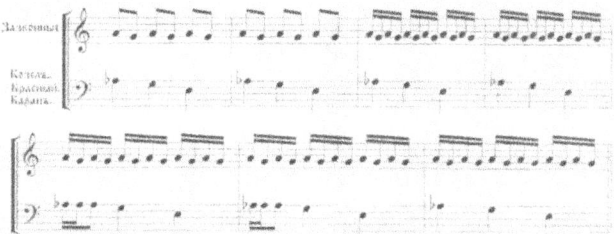

www.ingramcontent.com/pod-product-compliance
Lightning Source LLC
Chambersburg PA
CBHW061445300426
44114CB00014B/1850